Praise for

How to Thrive in the Virtual Workplace

"Robert Glazer has assembled an essential playbook both remote leaders and employees need to build top-tier organizations. This comprehensive book will help you set the right cultural foundation, hire effectively, and ensure top performance in remote work."

—Dr. Geoff Smart, chairman of ghSMART and *New York Times* bestselling author of *Who* and *Power Score*

"Robert Glazer, leader of a world-class, values-driven virtual organization, shares an important playbook to help employees, managers, and leaders build and excel in the new world of remote work."

—Garry Ridge, CEO of the WD-40 Company

"Robert Glazer has led a top performing remote organization for over a decade. With this book, he shares the essential keys to building a world-class remote company."

—Keith Ferrazzi, *New York Times* bestselling author of *Never Eat Alone*

"This is a must-read guide to excelling in the newly remote working world. Robert Glazer shares strategies to help leaders and workers unlock the transformative possibilities of remote work."

—Aicha Evans, CEO of Zoox

"Invaluable guidance on how organizations can embrace the flexibility of remote work while sustaining well-being and connection, from a trailblazing leader who has been doing this brilliantly for years. Immensely timely, practical, and encouraging."

—Caroline Webb, author of *How to Have a Good Day* and senior advisor to McKinsey & Company

HOW TO *Thrive* IN THE VIRTUAL WORKPLACE

Simple and Effective Tips for Successful, Productive, and Empowered Remote Work

ROBERT GLAZER
WITH MICK SLOAN

simple **truths**
▶ Small books. **BIG IMPACT.**

Published by Simple Truths, an imprint of Sourcebooks
P.O. Box 4410, Naperville, Illinois 60567-4410
(630) 961-3900
sourcebooks.com

Originally published as *How to Thrive in the Virtual Workplace* in 2021
in the United Kingdom by Bluebird, an imprint of Pan Macmillan. This
edition issued based on the paperback edition published in 2021 in the
United Kingdom by Bluebird, an imprint of Pan Macmillan.

Library of Congress Cataloging-in-Publication Data is on file with the publisher.

Printed and bound in the United States of America.
POD

Contents

Introduction

In 2017, our company, Acceleration Partners, made the decision to expand into the United Kingdom. One of the key decisions for our leadership team and our new managing director was how—and if—we could extend our remote working policy, which had existed for our American employees for over a decade and had become a foundation of our award-winning company culture, to the region.

At the time, working from home was even less common in the United Kingdom than it was in the United States, so our new managing director was understandably concerned that remote work would not be easily accepted by potential clients and employees.

Our experience with employees who worked remotely for

the first time when they joined our team was that they adjusted very quickly. However, we also understood the risks of entering a new market with a work style that went against traditional cultural norms. We ultimately reached a middle ground—securing a flex office space for our growing team to work together in person and to meet with prospective clients.

Then a funny thing happened. Within a few months, hardly anyone on the UK team was using the flex workspace. Even though remote work was new to all the employees in that region, they had all adapted quickly, and soon working from home had become their preference. Several of the UK team members enthusiastically communicated how much they appreciated being able to avoid their daily commute and shared that they could not see themselves ever returning to a full-time office environment.

Our global expansion experience illustrates what many companies have come to discover in their own remote work transitions. Some who have never experienced remote work wrongly assume it is untenable for their own organizations, and while remote work isn't for everyone, the reality—as many have come to learn—is that it's far more feasible than conventional wisdom might otherwise suggest.

Open Secret

For years, remote work has been gaining momentum, moving from a fringe business tactic to a model readily adopted both by employees and companies—even large, well-known organizations.

Even in the past decade, there has been a stigma surrounding remote work. People who hadn't experienced that workplace model pictured employees slacking off, lounging in their pajamas, and taking hours-long breaks throughout the workday.

Not only did this make prospective employees worry about working from home, it made clients and customers wary as well. Early in our company's history, we felt increased pressure to work exceptionally hard to prove we could deliver top-tier service even without an office. Some remote companies have even felt the need to hide their lack of an office from customers in order to appear more credible.

But times have changed, and this workplace model no longer needs to be a secret. Companies with remote work environments are more comfortable sharing the practice openly with clients and see it as an emerging competitive advantage to attract the best talent.

The United States has led the remote working revolution, with remote work growing by 44 percent in the past five years and 91 percent in the last ten.[1] However, the trend was beginning to catch on in other countries even before a global pandemic swept across the world in 2020 and forced nearly all companies to transition to remote work. And yet, despite having limited experience or preparation for that shift, a significant number of organizations found that for the most part, they were able to conduct business as usual. Many of their skeptical employees also found remote work far more agreeable than anticipated.

The Commuting Crunch

Long before the COVID-19 pandemic, the drawbacks of office life were becoming more apparent. The average American worker spent 225 hours, or nine days, commuting in 2019, and commute times have risen steadily over the past forty years.[2] The average commute in the United Kingdom is fifty-nine minutes *each way*.[3] In India, it's over two hours per day.[4] That's 7 percent of the entire day spent getting to and from work!

No matter where in the world people work, the commute keeps getting longer. This is especially true in areas where housing prices have continued to rise. In order to have an affordable place to call home, most workers have had to travel farther to get to work.

In most in-office organizations, the office environment doesn't help reduce stress and frustrations. The great open-plan workplace experiment of the past decade continues to be debunked from a productivity standpoint. One study by the *Guardian* found that employees in open-plan offices lose an average of eighty-six minutes per day to distractions, are 70 percent more likely than workers in traditional offices to take sick days, and are more likely to leave the office earlier in the day.[5] This adds up to a status quo where employees spend more time than ever commuting to work and get less done while they're there.

This is not a positive or productive trend, which is why when millions of workers around the world were abruptly forced to work remotely from home, most employees were far more open to it than their employers may have realized. Although COVID-19 triggered the largest remote work experiment in history, on a global scale, nonetheless, there's every reason to believe this new work-from-home reality will continue. Companies as large as Twitter have already told employees they never have to return to the office if they don't want to.[6] Moreover, I believe the organizations that can build a thriving culture in a remote workplace will be the leaders of tomorrow and will attract the best talent.

A Competitive Advantage

When I started Acceleration Partners in 2007, the decision to make our workforce 100 percent remote was initially an attempt to preemptively solve a pain point.

We are a specialized agency in a segment of digital marketing known as affiliate or partner marketing. In this model, brands partner with individuals or companies (referred to as affiliates, partners, and publishers) and pay them on a performance basis for delivering desired outcomes. It's an area of business that has grown considerably over the past decade but was more niche at the time, with small and diffuse pockets of talent.

We were winning large accounts and needed experienced account managers from the industry—talent that was scattered all over the country. There simply wasn't enough experienced and available affiliate program management talent in any single city. We assumed remote working would be a temporary solution, but we enjoyed the competitive advantage and flexibility it provided our company, as did our employees.

Building our team by hiring remote employees from across the United States allowed us to access a far larger talent pool than in-office organizations forced to hire within a geographic area. By committing to a remote strategy, we were able to hire the people we needed and offer them a flexible working style that increased retention and satisfaction.

This is an advantage that companies around the world can emulate, especially businesses that service clients or customers in multiple regions. As today's technology makes it possible for organizations in a wide variety of industries to operate with dispersed, remote employees, it's logical that companies around the world would use that capability to seek and acquire the best talent, irrespective of location.

For example, although our global expansion initially started in the UK, we leveraged our model to hire employees from across Europe to better service our clients in multiple countries. Those hires were easier and faster to onboard because we didn't need to first invest in an office in each market we serviced.

A More Even Playing Field

Hiring remote employees can also be an important step toward building more equitable workplaces. The reality is that the cost of living in cities such as New York, San Francisco, and London is prohibitive for many professionals, especially younger ones already saddled with student debt. The current norm of in-person offices in expensive hub cities tends to benefit those with more resources at their disposal. This presents a particular issue for people of color in the workforce, who often face economic disadvantages relative to their white counterparts. For example, in the United States, the average Black or Latino family owns under $7,000 in wealth, as compared to the $147,000 in wealth held by the average white family.[7] This wealth disparity manifests itself in more student debt, less access to higher-priced housing, and more dire consequences for taking entrepreneurial risks. When companies aren't limited to a talent pool in an expensive urban hub, it opens career opportunities for a wider range of people, regardless of their economic background.

While the ability to hire diverse pockets of talent is one great benefit of the remote work model, offering flexibility to employees is another crucial factor. The changing conversation and expectations around work-life flexibility continue to erode the appeal of a traditional, full-time office job.

There's been a global shift in how we talk about work-life integration. Increasingly, workers want more flexibility and autonomy; they want to be able to travel and have more personal and family time and even the freedom to launch their own side hustle. The rise of the gig economy has also increased job liquidity and expanded availability of contract work that isn't geographically dependent.

In the United States alone, there are six million more gig workers today than a decade ago. Three million of those people reflect the shift of the labor force toward this type of work and away from more traditional employment.[8]

These are talented people who might otherwise be looking for full-time work in areas where they would have fewer options available. They are also prospective employees who can simply opt out of the workforce, choosing instead to dictate how and when they work if the alternative is not attractive.

Organizations that offer remote work can excel by appealing to this exact group of people. If flexibility is becoming an increasingly desirable workplace trait, flexible and remote work is the best way to meet that need in a sustainable way.

Remote Works

One distinct advantage that organizations have today is that the remote model is more accepted than ever. Ten years ago, remote employees had to overcome the misperception that instead of productively working, they were focused on caring for their young children, watching television, running personal errands, or otherwise being unaccountable for their time and schedule.

It took years for remote organizations to overcome these external biases and prove they could deliver a high level of service without an office. The image in many people's heads of employees slacking off at home has been replaced by a track record of strong performance and results. The early adopters of remote work walked so the virtual businesses of today can run.

If you're considering joining a remote organization as an employee, starting a remote business as an entrepreneur, or making your team permanently remote, you're starting in a much better position than the organizations that came before you.

Creating a high-performance, remote work culture isn't easy, but organizations that commit to doing it with the proper foundation, playbook, and procedures can reap exponential benefits. I know this from our experience at Acceleration Partners. Since we decided to go all in on remote culture in 2011, we've grown over 1,000 percent in ten years and expanded our team to almost two hundred employees across eight countries. We have won multiple "best place to work" awards even though we don't have luxurious offices, Ping-Pong tables in the break room, or in-office baristas and masseuses. Clearly, these "perks" are not what makes a great culture, though in some cases, companies try to use these sorts of fringe benefits to cover up a poor work environment and encourage people to never leave the office.

Instead of prioritizing investments in a physical setting, we can focus on investing in our team members—personally and professionally. Because we are not interacting in person with one another on a daily basis, we excel by hiring people who value independence and flexibility, and we invest in their development from day one. That is a key skill set for the virtual working environment. We've even developed most of our own leaders—80 percent of people in leadership roles at Acceleration Partners have been promoted from within.

Remote work is the new frontier for the business world. I know from firsthand experience that remote work, when done effectively, drives greater happiness and engagement for employees and is a key competitive advantage.

A Roadmap for This Book

Here's what you can expect.

First, we'll start at the employee level. We'll explore the unique challenges, solutions, and rewards of remote working and ways to ensure you're happy, engaged, and productive while working virtually. Knowing that so many people have been forced unwittingly into remote work by COVID-19, we'll also dig into what you can expect if you find yourself working virtually beyond the pandemic.

Then, we'll discuss the organizational playbook that business leaders can use to build a world-class remote culture. We'll examine the structural principles needed for any top remote culture, including understanding what that culture is and how the right cultural foundation enables and supports remote work.

From there, we'll dive into the specific strategies to apply in a remote environment. Most employees and businesses can and will excel while working from home if they have the right systems and processes in place. However, the same procedures and tactics that are often used in an office should not be applied in a virtual setting if one hopes to realize optimal results.

Depending on your role, you may be tempted to dive right into the first part of this book, thriving as a remote employee, which helps you learn how to better navigate the remote workplace. Or you may be inclined to skip directly to the next section, thriving as a remote organization, which tackles the leadership and management aspects of remote work. Feel free to skip around, but the reality is that most of us will soon find ourselves on both sides of the remote work coin.

PART ONE

Thriving
as a Remote
Employee

1

Remote Working: What's It All About?

When Sophie Parry-Billings decided to start working remotely, everyone she knew was alarmed.

"Everyone I told—my family, my friends, my boyfriend—were all really worried about me working remotely," Parry-Billings said in explaining her decision. "Because I'm just such a people person. I love being around people."

Parry-Billings has worked for Acceleration Partners since 2017, serving as our associate director of marketing in Europe, the Middle East, and Africa. Before joining our team, she had never worked remotely, even on a part-time basis. On top of that, she lived (and still lives) in London, where working from home was essentially unheard of in the business world at the time.

Parry-Billings's peers were certain she'd feel isolated working from home, especially because she'd be the only person in her social circle doing so. But even though she had no experience with virtual work, she had an inescapable feeling that she'd enjoy it. So she took the plunge.

Although she'd had good experiences working in an office in the past, Parry-Billings's most recent office job was a maddening environment reminiscent of a new age workplace parody. She spent six months working in a large open-plan office, sharing a floor with fifty colleagues, working at long tables, and dealing with endless distractions.

"I hated that office. It was loud, it was cliquey, and they played music all the time," Parry-Billings recalled. "There was literally a Sonos speaker next to my desk, and I had no control over whether it was on or off."

On top of that, Parry-Billings spent ninety minutes commuting daily, cramming onto the London Underground twice a day just to get to this distracting work environment. She was living an all-too-familiar unpleasant office experience, unaware that there were better workplace models available.

Even after her last experience, Parry-Billings didn't actively seek out a virtual role when she joined our team. London has an ingrained office culture, where commuting into the city, going out for drinks after work, and going straight from work to the club on a Friday night is quite common. Remote work was so rare in the UK in 2017 that people outside the company were stunned when Parry-Billings joined video calls from a home office. She was taking a chance and stepping onto a professional frontier when she started working virtually.

And yet, despite being an extrovert in one of the least virtual-work-oriented cities in the world, Parry-Billings adjusted quickly, and she has loved working from home ever since.

Parry-Billings especially loves having the ability to set a flexible schedule for herself, allowing her to focus on her health, wellness, and personal relationships without sacrificing her work. When she worked in an office, she often left for work particularly early to avoid peak hours on the Underground. She ate a rushed lunch at her desk and would often eat junk food for dinner, simply because she was too exhausted from a full day of working and commuting to prepare anything else.

Since transitioning to remote work, Parry-Billings has enjoyed, in her words, "a drastically better quality of life." She can make space in her schedule to exercise and cook healthy meals. She can set aside extended blocks of time for quiet, focused work without worrying about loud colleagues or blaring music. She can even visit family who live in other cities more frequently and for more extended stays.

"Before, if I wanted to see them for an extended period of time, I would have to take a day off," Parry-Billings said.

"Whereas now, I can work on the train and work at my parents' house. I can spend more time with my family than if I was visiting them for one night over a weekend."

Parry-Billings acknowledges that her remote work experience isn't perfect. London isn't known for offering spacious homes, and when she first started working from home, she had to keep her desk in her bedroom, as it was the only space she had available. She initially faced challenges separating her work and home lives, including struggling to set a clear time to stop working at the end of the day. While the benefits of virtual work outweigh any drawbacks in her eyes, there were some adjustments, even during nonpandemic times.

She emphasized that it was helpful that she joined a completely remote organization rather than being one of a small number of virtual employees at an otherwise in-person company. We knew that virtual work wouldn't be an established norm for our European team members, so we made a specific effort to make the onboarding process as smooth as possible for them and gave them resources for a smooth adjustment.

As a manager, Parry-Billings has helped multiple direct reports adapt to a flexible working environment. Our organization tends to attract conscientious, highly accountable people, and managers occasionally have to remind employees that they have the freedom to design a schedule that works for them, as long as they accomplish their tasks and communicate clearly with clients and colleagues. In the early days of working from home, Parry-Billings needed some encouragement in this regard herself.

"When I first started, it took a bit of a while to get in the groove of how flexible I was allowed to be," Parry-Billings recalled. "I would ping my manager, say, 'hey, I'm going to do a workout.' And she would say, 'you don't need to tell me that, it's fine.' That was her way of doing it."

Trust is a foundational element of any positive work environment. This is especially true for remote organizations. Parry-Billings's story illustrates that remote work is most beneficial for employees when they are given the trust and autonomy to leverage the flexibility that can come from working from home.

Of course, employees need to hold up their end of the bargain as well. Remote work isn't an opportunity for employees to do whatever they want, take days off on a whim, or work in bed all day. Working virtually will be difficult if you aren't accountable to your colleagues, don't dedicate yourself to getting your tasks done in an unstructured, unsupervised environment, and expect to excel without taking care to set up an appropriate, professional workspace for yourself.

"You have to be a really disciplined person," Parry-Billings advised. "You have to be able to manage your schedule, and you have to be able to focus while not in an office."

Essentially, the formula for successful remote work is simple: take workers who are dedicated, disciplined, and accountable, and put them in a trusting environment with well-established processes and good cultural principles.

The fact is the organization you work for partially dictates how fulfilled you'll be working from home. From an employee's perspective, remote work is immensely more rewarding when you are part of an organization that has a healthy culture, dedicated, collaborative employees, and well-established best practices. Remote work isn't something that any company can successfully transition to overnight, as Parry-Billings saw her friends learn when the COVID-19 pandemic suddenly forced most UK businesses to start working from home without the right systems.

But with the proper environment, structures, systems, and principles in place, the possibilities are immense for remote employees. The fact is, no matter where they work, there are steps that workers can take to maximize their professional effectiveness, personal happiness, and overall fulfillment while working from home.

As for Parry-Billings, she barely misses the office at all. Despite the fears of her friends and family, she has learned that virtual work can yield both anticipated and unexpected benefits.

"I feel like I just surprised everyone and really enjoyed it," Parry-Billings said with a laugh.

The Remote Work Foundation

I've shared that there are some misconceptions about remote work, including the belief that virtual employees are less productive. There's an incorrect assumption that people who work from home are not accountable and let their homelife distractions spill into their work.

What we and many other organizations have actually found is that the opposite is more often the case. When employees struggle with spillover, it tends to flow in the opposite direction. For example, some employees find it difficult to set boundaries that separate their work life from their personal life when they work remotely. They struggle to unplug, take breaks, recharge, and decompress at the end of the workday. Sometimes they even struggle to end their workday, checking their email late and leaving their laptop on their bedside table so they can check email one last time before bed.

Research during COVID-19 supports this. Employees who began working from home during the pandemic were twice as likely to send messages after traditional work hours as they struggled to disconnect from their jobs.[1]

To address this challenge, remote organizations must instill in all their employees—from an entry-level associate to members of the executive team—the importance of setting a solid foundation for remote work, maintaining a schedule, creating the right physical workspace, and setting professional and personal boundaries.

As with most things, a crucial step to success in remote work is putting yourself in the best possible environment, with the correct tools, from the outset. If you step into remote work by digging up the laptop you used in college and with the mindset of working from the couch all day, you'll quickly find yourself frustrated and fatigued.

Technology

To start, you will want to ensure you have the hardware and technological capabilities needed to succeed. If you're frequently on video calls with clients or regularly uploading or sending large files, it's important to ensure your technology won't slow down your productivity.

This starts with your internet connection. While a majority of people have high-speed internet today, speeds can vary dramatically, so it's important to ensure you have the correct specifications. Most providers tout the download speed that an internet plan offers in their marketing, but upload speed is equally important for users who frequently use video calls or upload materials to cloud storage. Don't assume your internet's upload and download speeds are equal—it's common for internet providers to offer excellent download speed but lower upload speed. Most organizations recommend upload and download speeds of at least 25 megabits per second for a single user. If you have multiple devices or other heavy internet users, that number goes up quickly.

Many internet service providers offer fast, free speed testing of your network and device. The widely used tool Speedtest by Ookla also offers free, instant speed testing. If your upload or download speed leaves something to be desired, it's worth contacting your internet service provider to see what faster options are available.

FREE SPEED TESTING RESOURCES

► Ookla Speedtest—speedtest.net

► Fast—fast.com

► PC Mag—pcm-intl.speedtestcustom.com[2]

Number of Devices	Use Cases	Recommended Download Speed
1–2	Web surfing, email, social networking, moderate video	Up to 25 Mbps
3–5	Online multiplayer gaming, 4K streaming	50–100 Mbps
More than 5	All of the above plus sharing large files and live streaming video	150–200 Mbps

Employees should ask managers and companies for guidance on any specifications on the laptop processing power, disc storage space, and wireless speed that is necessary to meet company standards, keeping in mind that laptops that are used heavily seem to start to degrade in performance after two to three years. Some companies provide a document outlining the minimum technology requirements needed to do the job.

Here is an example of the guidelines we provide for new employees. We update them annually.

REQUIRED OPERATING SYSTEMS

Windows

Windows 10 64-bit Professional required (Windows Home version does not include required security capabilities).

If you are going to be using an existing computer with Windows 10 Home version, upgrades to the Professional or Business version are available from Microsoft.

RECOMMENDED COMPUTER HARDWARE— MINIMUM SPECIFICATIONS

Windows

→ Processor: Intel i5 (minimum requirement)

→ Memory: 8 GB RAM minimum (we suggest 16 GB RAM for increased performance)

→ Disk space: 256 GB SSD hard drive (512 GB is even better) is highly recommended

RECOMMENDED NETWORK EQUIPMENT AND BANDWIDTH

Wireless Standard

→ Wireless standard 802.11x (n/ac preferred)

Bandwidth

→ At least 25 Mbps of internet speed upload/download (faster is better)

Wireless Equipment (Router)

→ Any modern wireless equipment will work

Optional but highly recommended: Add 2- or 3-year extended warranty (example: Dell Pro Support onsite next day, etc.).

Setting the Stage

With the explosion of video conferencing, it's likely that you'll spend a significant amount of time online when remote working in your own version of a mini stage—occasionally with a large audience. There are several worthwhile accessories that you should consider from the outset to help you be more productive and look more professional.

Especially in roles where you are externally facing, such as sales, executive leadership, or client services, it's important to appear as professional as possible. Even as it becomes more natural to join a video call with someone working at home, if your workspace is dark and disorganized or it's difficult to hear you, it can send the wrong impression to people outside your company—or to your new boss.

First impressions matter. Here are some suggestions and resources to help ensure you're making a good one in your virtual work environment.

SECOND MONITOR

Having a second monitor can be very helpful as it allows you to use more programs at once, compare and contrast materials, and avoid the problem of hunching over a laptop all day.

HEADSET/HEADPHONES

For video calls, you should always use a headset, be it earbuds or an actual headset with a microphone built in, rather than relying on the built-in speaker in your computer. Some prefer over-the-ear headsets with a microphone connected, others use Bluetooth earbuds such as Apple AirPods, and others simply use the built-in microphone on their computer with inexpensive earbuds. The point is to use something other than the built-in speakers in your laptop when communicating with others on a work call. The built-in computer speakers often pick up your room noise and result in "noise bleed" when the audio from the person you're speaking with comes through your speakers and gets picked up by your microphone, resulting in a distracting echo. So you hear them, but they also hear themselves at the same time, which is not ideal.

A GOOD CAMERA

Most laptops these days have good built-in cameras, but it can also be worth buying an inexpensive HD webcam that you can clip onto your monitor. Or, you can have your camera freestanding on a camera stand, which may offer better video clarity or control over the location and angle. Logitech has some great models.

GOOD LIGHTING

Room lighting is an often overlooked factor in remote work communication. There are several inexpensive lights you can buy that go next to your laptop or even clip on the screen that can make a noticeable difference in your appearance. Ring lights aren't just for Instagram influencers—they're an affordable, easy way to ensure great lighting for your day-to-day calls. You may also find it helpful to incorporate natural light into your workspace, both to improve your lighting on video calls and also to add a pleasant atmosphere to your workspace. If you are able to have your workspace in a room with a window, that can go a long way toward making your home office feel more welcoming.

WORK STATION OR STANDING DESK

For the sake of your long-term comfort while working from home, it's important to ensure that your workspace is a place where you are comfortable working for long periods of time. You could consider investing in an ergonomic desk chair that will be more comfortable to sit in during a long workday, or you may even choose to purchase an adjustable standing desk, which allows you to stand for extended periods of time while you work.

PROFESSIONAL BACKGROUND

Ideally, the background that shows up when you're on a video call should be clean and free of clutter and should establish that you are in a professionally organized space, even in your home. While working from home is becoming more normal, it could send the wrong message if an unmade bed with a pile of dirty clothes on it appears in the background when you join a video call.

Many video-call applications offer virtual backgrounds. However, depending on your lighting and setup, these could create an odd effect where parts of your body keep disappearing and reappearing during the call, which could be more of a distraction. So test it out before settling on a virtual background.

If you are an executive or are in a role where you have frequent, high-leverage video calls and don't have a clean background setting, I would strongly suggest purchasing a green screen. This option significantly improves the efficacy of virtual backgrounds and allows you to maintain a professional appearance no matter what's going on in your home. After struggling with a vinyl background that took up too much space when not in use, I finally found a collapsible green screen for $200 that retracts into its case on the floor for efficient storage. My virtual office looks so real that I'm often asked about the items in my background when I'm on calls.

There are cheaper green screen options as well, including simple cloth versions. Most video-conference platforms now have a green screen option in their video settings, and the background quality is noticeably better.

BLUE LIGHT GLASSES

Finally, you may consider investing in glasses that filter out blue light from your computer screen. Depending on your vision needs, you can get these either with prescription lenses or without. Wearing glasses that filter out blue light can help protect you from eyestrain when you are staring at a screen all day and have also been connected to higher-quality sleep when worn in the evening.[3]

Many remote organizations will offer a home-office stipend that can reimburse you for these types of improvements. However, even if your organization doesn't reimburse for some or all of these, they can be acquired for an affordable price—certainly for less than the money you'll save by not commuting to the office—and will put you in a better position to succeed.

Getting the technology that you need together is just part of the transition to remote working. Adjusting your mindset is also vital for fully embracing this new way of working and thriving with the myriad benefits that it brings.

TECHNOLOGY RESOURCES CHECKLIST

Basics/Essentials

→ Wireless internet standard of 802.11x

→ At least 25 Mbps of upload speed and download speed—
   don't assume these are the same

→ Laptop with a built-in webcam, 8 GB RAM, 256 GB SSD hard
   drive

→ Headset with built-in microphone or headphones with separate microphone

Nice to Have

→ Second monitor

→ Laptop stand

→ Separate keyboard or mouse

→ HD webcam

→ Blue light blocking glasses

Advanced/Luxuries

→ Ring light or light box

→ Green screen background

→ Standing desk

2

Getting the Most out of Remote Work

In this chapter, we'll delve into how virtual employees can lay an effective foundation for themselves, fully leverage the flexibility of remote work to benefit themselves personally and professionally, and stay motivated, focused, and engaged. Along the way, you'll hear from other employees who have worked remotely for years—pre- and postpandemic—and made remarkable, lasting changes to their lives as a result.

Setting Expectations

If you're working remotely for the first time, it's essential to set expectations for your new colleagues about when you are and aren't working. While everybody deviates slightly from day to day, it's helpful to clarify to your manager and coworkers if, for instance, you prefer to work from 9:00 a.m. to 6:00 p.m. each day with an hour at 12:00 p.m. for lunch.

What you don't want is to be unreachable when people expect you to be working. Nothing erodes trust faster in a virtual working environment than when someone is unavailable or can't be found easily at a time at which they have designated they will be working.

For example, we had a situation where an employee was not upfront about not having childcare during key working hours—a necessity we explicitly discussed in the recruiting process—and the situation was clearly impacting their availability and quality of work. When their manager reached out to the employee and had a frank discussion about their subpar performance, this underlying problem was revealed. The manager expressed their dismay that the employee had not been forthcoming about the situation, sharing that they could have worked together on a solution. Ultimately, the employee resigned, realizing there had been a breach of trust with the team that was likely irreparable.

Being able to set a flexible schedule is one of the keystone benefits of remote work, especially for working parents, but it's important not to take advantage of that flexibility. Unless you're dealing with an unexpected school closure or illness, you shouldn't attempt to juggle work and nonwork responsibilities at the same time. It is especially inadvisable to attempt to parent and work at the same time; doing so will drastically decrease your ability to do either effectively. There is a significant difference between choosing remote work because of the flexibility it gives you for your family (i.e., schedule, hours, pickup and drop-off options) and trying to do both simultaneously.

Set your schedule, and communicate this to your team. This will help ensure you have quality, uninterrupted, guilt-free time inside and outside work.

The Pandemic Paradigm

The COVID-19 pandemic unfortunately meant that most people's first remote work experience came alongside unprecedented school closures and sudden loss of childcare coverage. This has led to more grace and understanding from employers and other colleagues, but it should not be the norm when things are back to the new normal and a far larger number of people are working from home.

The good news is that if you are a working parent who excelled at remote work during the pandemic, you will likely enjoy and appreciate it even more when you aren't forced to juggle your parenting responsibilities simultaneously. Here's an example of how to set these expectations with new employees.

WORK CULTURE AND ENVIRONMENT

The virtual working environment at Acceleration Partners offers all employees the opportunity for great flexibility. We have very high expectations for performance while believing in the value of family and personal objectives. As an employee of Acceleration Partners, you have the flexibility to make your own work-life balance by owning your calendar, planning in advance, and communicating effectively.

If you are away or unavailable during standard working hours, please let your manager know, schedule your time in your calendar, and communicate with your teammates so they may plan accordingly. Please work with your manager to discuss expectations on availability.

"Great leaders understand that life is dynamic and the best organizations accommodate their teams' lives and shift constantly to make it work."

EXPECTATIONS FOR ALL EMPLOYEES

→ Ask questions, ask for help, and ask for clarity.

→ Have a problem-solving orientation and come with solutions. If you can't figure it out in a reasonable amount of time—refer to #1.

→ Communicate when you will be online and offline.

→ Take long vacations and take short vacations.

→ Take clarity breaks and know when to unplug. He-man/she-man hours are not rewarded.

→ Use the Slack channel with the hashtag #commit_to_3 to focus on three daily priorities.

→ Speak up and bring solutions when something (process/task/etc.) is not right or you can make it better.

→ Take initiative—make this your own experience.

→ Give feedback and cheers for peers via TINYpulse.

→ Use your best judgment always, and we will back you up when needed.

→ When/if Acceleration Partners is no longer right for you and you are no longer happy, it is okay and expected that we can have an open conversation about it. We will try to fix it first, and if we can't, we will help you on your path to a better fit. Out of the blue two-week notice is frowned upon—please give us the opportunity to fix it first.

Information from the Acceleration Partners welcome guide.

Remote Reflections: Like a Fish to Water

Some employees enter remote work with a certain degree of trepidation. Even if you are looking forward to avoiding a commute or enjoy working in quiet solitude, it's natural to wonder, on some level, if you will actually be happy working in such a drastically different environment. This is especially true for people who have only worked in traditional office jobs throughout their career to date.

But conversely, some people just know they will love remote work and have proactively sought out these types of opportunities throughout their careers. As you'll see, Tess Waresmith is one of the best examples of this type of person. Waresmith has been on our team since 2016, currently serving as our director of business operations. Although Acceleration Partners is her first full-time remote role, she has worked remotely throughout her career beforehand. In fact, Waresmith's last office-only role was her college internship. That was all the experience she needed to know that nine-to-five office life wasn't for her.

Waresmith felt trapped by the rigid structure of in-office work. She didn't like having to arrive at nine and leave at five every day, and she especially didn't like working in the dimly lit, windowless office. Before formally launching her career, she realized she was better suited to the flexibility and possibility of virtual work.

Waresmith's first experience working from home came in a three-year stint in a hybrid organization. The company was small, and while they had an office, leadership was relaxed about how many days per week employees had to be physically present. Waresmith immediately noticed that working from home allowed her to be more productive, more fulfilled, and even more motivated.

In fact, Waresmith believes that having the opportunity to work in a flexible environment has driven her to deliver the best possible results.

"I have always had a sense of gratitude while working remotely," she said. "I always felt compelled to do a good job because I was able to, for example, go skiing before I came into the office or work from the mountains so I could go for a hike on a Friday. I never took remote work for granted from the very beginning, because I'd had that one in-office experience as an intern that I didn't really like."

From the beginning of her virtual experience, Waresmith has always used the flexibility of remote work to prioritize her personal passions. Most notably, she used the ability to set her own schedule to maintain her status as a highly competitive athlete, competing in USA Weightlifting as a nationally ranked weightlifter. Top athletic performance requires consistent training, and Waresmith was able to build extended gym sessions into her daily work routine, allowing her to stay on top of her game without sacrificing her professional progress.

Needless to say, this type of training schedule would be difficult to maintain alongside a traditional office job. Most of us have faced the same exercise conundrum in our own lives: Do we wake up before dawn to work out before work, or do we attempt to exercise after leaving the office, when we're hungry for dinner and sluggish after a long day of sitting at our desk? Neither option is ideal for many of us, and we too often end up neglecting our health as a result.

Waresmith didn't have this problem; she made a habit of starting work early, then hitting the gym as an extended break after a few hours of work. She got her required training out of the way and returned to her home office feeling accomplished and refreshed.

Waresmith is an avid traveler, and she is a firm believer that changing your environment from time to time benefits your personal fulfillment and your professional output. She has taken multiple long trips without missing work; she is now based in the Boston area, having spent extended periods of time working for Acceleration Partners in places as distant as Singapore and New Zealand.

Waresmith always clears these trips with her manager, having ensured her destinations and accommodations would have strong internet and a good space to work. She understands that part of the flexible lifestyle afforded by working virtually means taking care to hold up your end of the bargain. That's why she strongly recommends being as clear as possible when setting expectations for both your managers and your colleagues when working remotely.

Some companies still rely on command and control leadership that requires employees to be constantly available at certain degrees of time. But increasingly, more organizations are predominantly concerned with making sure employees are able to get their work done and make themselves available with a high degree of consistency. Waresmith has found that when organizations trust employees to do their jobs, regardless of when or where they work, workers appreciate that trust and respond by giving their best effort.

Waresmith can also speak to the virtual management experience, as she currently leads a team of five and has managed at least one direct report since 2017. As part of the role, she has helped others acclimatize to working from home, including people who were less certain the workplace model was the right fit for them.

"I always tell people to be very conscious of your calendar," Waresmith said. "Have direct conversations with your manager about what works for you. If working nine-to-five online all day works for you, great. If there are adjustments you can make to make your work life easier, tell your manager how you want to adjust. As long as you're available for your clients and your team, it's okay to adjust your schedule. Just let us know what your day looks like."

Remote work is most effective when these types of

transparent communications take place upfront. When remote employees show their managers that they reliably accomplish their tasks and deliver top-tier work for customers, clients, and colleagues, that commitment earns a great degree of trust, respect, and flexibility. And setting clear expectations about availability is the best way to create an arrangement that works for everyone.

While Waresmith adapted to remote work more naturally than the average person, she generally believes most people can find fulfillment working virtually, even if they have doubts or concerns. People who need rigid structure are more likely to gravitate toward office life, but that doesn't mean it's impossible to have a structured workday while working from home. As Waresmith noted above, employees who want to work from nine to five every day in a virtual workplace are more than welcome to do so.

It helps to be someone like Waresmith, for whom personal activities such as world-class weightlifting and global travel are top priorities in a well-balanced life. But Waresmith doesn't think an affinity for flexibility is an inherent trait that some of us simply don't possess. Rather, she believes people enjoy that aspect of working from home more than they'd expect.

"People don't know what they don't know," Waresmith said. "And if people have worked their entire life in an office, they might feel like they need that interpersonal option and that structure to be successful. But they might not really need that."

To the interpersonal point, it's notable that Waresmith has developed what she considers lifelong friendships with her remote colleagues. While she acknowledges it takes a bit of additional effort to create these connections, relationship building forms a crucial part of remote work. Employees don't need to choose between working from home and building lasting relationships with colleagues—it's entirely possible to do both.

While people like Waresmith are perhaps more likely to adapt quickly to virtual work, don't assume that it is wrong for you, especially if your only experience of doing it is under the stress of the pandemic. Even if you don't crave or need flexibility, there's a good chance that the opportunity to set your own schedule and work from different locations will bring benefits you wouldn't necessarily expect.

Setting Physical Boundaries

The most obvious benefit of working in an office is the physical delineation between personal and professional life. A real concern that many face when working remotely is that it will feel like they live at their office and they won't be able to create the separation they need to rest and relax outside work.

It's very possible to mitigate this spillover effect, but it requires setting careful physical boundaries to separate your work from your home life. If it's possible to do so, it's important to have a place in your home that is specifically designated for work. This not only helps you mentally delineate work time, but it also signals to other people in your home when you're available and when you're not.

This is especially essential for people who live with others—be it a roommate, a partner, children, or other family members. Without that clear working/not working signal, it's understandable that those in your household will think that because you are visible, you're available. They might be tempted to walk in and ask you a question without realizing you're in the middle of a sales pitch or on a client call.

It can be hard for others to realize you're working before it's too late, but setting aside a designated space for work helps avoid this confusion. For most employees, physical separation is easier said than done, especially for people who weren't expecting to be working from home. Not everyone has a room in their home they can designate as an office. In those cases, even setting up a folding table in the corner of the living room or selecting a chair at the kitchen table as an "office chair" is an important step toward creating a mental and physical boundary. Those delineations can also help you to exit work mode when you remove yourself from that space at the end of the workday.

Keeping a Schedule

It's vital to keep a structured schedule and be intentional about how time is used. It's helpful for employees working outside the office to set a consistent wakeup time, determine what range of hours they'll be working during the day, and proactively plan what time is reserved for projects and meetings, lunch, exercise, and personal time. It's similarly essential to schedule breaks into the day and stick to those break times.

When people work in an in-office environment, there are several ways in which breaks are naturally built in, such as chatting with coworkers at the watercooler, taking a coffee break, or going out to pick up lunch. In contrast, remote employees can easily burrow into their work for several hours without even realizing how much of the day has passed.

By setting a schedule and following it, you'll be better positioned to ensure you have time to get your work done but also that you take time to rest and reset during the day. Teams can even synchronize their schedules so all members of a team are doing fully focused work at the same times, which limits disruption within the group.

Awareness around the importance of schedule setting was heightened during COVID-19, most notably for working parents with kids at home. The working parents who adjusted best were those who coordinated their schedules with their partner or spouse, determining in advance who would be with the kids at which times, clarifying when one partner absolutely has to be working, and other similar steps.

Managing Your Inbox

Email is often the first communication option that employees turn to in virtual settings, when quick in-person communication is off the table. If you're working remotely for the first time, it's fair to expect your email volume will increase substantially, as extended electronic exchanges replace short conversations over an office cubicle wall or across the table in an open-office environment. Instant messaging platforms like Slack and Microsoft Teams can help cut down on emails. However, they can also create a communication channel that employees compulsively check throughout the day, distracting them from focused, uninterrupted work.

Some experts have even suggested that remote employees are more likely to push tasks off their overcrowded plates by assigning the work to others via email or messaging platforms. Cal Newport, a distinguished professor, *New York Times* bestselling author of *Deep Work: Rules for Focused Success in a Distracted World*, and researcher on workplace productivity, clarified this point in a recent essay in the *New Yorker*, saying, "In person, for instance, the social cost of asking someone to take on a task is amplified; this friction gives colleagues reason to be thoughtful about the number of tasks they pass off to others. In a remote workplace, in which coworkers are reduced to abstract email addresses or Slack handles, it's easier for them to overload each other in an effort to declare victory over their own rapidly filling inboxes."[1]

Under these conditions, it's possible for workers on virtual teams to be bombarded with emails throughout the day, especially those in external-facing roles such as client services, who take in messages from both coworkers and customers.

Constantly checking and responding to emails throughout the day is not good for stress levels or productivity. That said, it's also not reasonable to just ignore your email inbox indefinitely. To strike a balance, there are tactics that can be used to allow for responsiveness without allowing email to control your day.

Time blocking. One option is to designate small blocks of time each day that are specifically for responding to email. For example, you may decide to respond to emails for thirty to sixty minutes at the beginning and end of each day. As long as you set that expectation with people who need to reach you most often and provide an alternate way to contact you in case of an emergency, this is a way to avoid constant email monitoring without leaving your team in the lurch.

Natural selection. If the idea of completely closing your email for most of the work day seems inadvisable for your role, one strategy we recommend to new employees is to be selective about which emails they respond to immediately and which they save for later. If an email is particularly time-sensitive or can be replied to in less than a minute, it may be best to respond to those immediately to get them out of the way. However, if you receive an email during the day that requires a detailed or careful response, it's perhaps better to save that for one of your designated email response time blocks or move it to a follow-up folder.

Setting expectations. If you manage a team, it's also helpful to suggest this strategy to them. You can even set a standard for every team member to follow, such as requesting that all emails that require a response should be replied to within twenty-four hours. For our client services team, we even create a separate email address for urgent issues, so these will rise to the top of the inbox. Anything that doesn't fall into the urgent category is fine to respond to later, within the twenty-four-hour window.

Email sorting. If you are worried about missing urgent messages during periods when you aren't responding to email and looking for a way to separate what's urgent from the noise, consider investing in an email management tool. There are several such plug-ins that use machine learning to automatically filter out promotional emails and those that are less important into a folder that you can then check only a couple of times per day or sort those that are marked as "urgent" or "important" into a special folder to keep your eye on.

If you use one of these systems, you don't need to watch your inbox throughout the day. All you need to do is check your urgent/important folder to make sure you don't miss those crucial messages.

If you use one of these plug-ins, your inbox will feel a lot less overwhelming when you open your email. One of my favorites is SaneBox, a tool I have used for over five years and that works with any email application. It automatically filters nonurgent emails into a "Sane Later" folder. It also has a feature where I can schedule emails to bounce back to my inbox after a set period of time if they warrant a response or follow-up. Tools like SaneBox dramatically reduce the overwhelming sensation when you see an inbox crushed with new messages every time you open your email and limit the number of notifications you get if you have email notifications on your smartphone.

Like many aspects of work, the most ineffective strategy for managing your inbox is the lack of a strategy. If you take an intentional approach to controlling your email rather than allowing a constant flow of messages to dictate your workday, you'll find yourself getting more done and feeling less stressed.

Managing Your Energy

Keeping yourself from overworking isn't just about managing when you work, it's also about how you work and what you do when. Just because you have certain hours designated for work during the day doesn't mean you should drill into intense, uninterrupted work for hours at a time. When you build your schedule, it's good to mix and match different types of activities, along with breaks, and to notice when your energy peaks and wanes.

In the fitness world, there's a widespread practice of interval training: strong bursts of rigorous exercise followed by a brief period of rest. This builds your strength and stamina without overexerting your body. Interval training can be applied to mental tasks as well, separating periods of mentally strenuous work with short breaks to ensure you don't burn out.

Personally, I like to schedule periods of intense work in the morning—when I am cognitively strongest—for tasks that involve writing and development of new materials. Then I'll follow that with a break and reserve the afternoon for meetings and tasks that are discussion-oriented and don't require as much mental capacity.

It's important to set a similar regimen for yourself and spend some time deciding which parts of the day are best for you to perform different types of tasks. This may take some trial and error, but determining what works for you will have a long-lasting impact on your happiness and productivity.

Creating Workday Buffers

On a similar theme, it's incredibly helpful to have buffer activities that help delineate work time from personal time. There's a natural instinct for remote employees to hop on their phone or work computer as soon as they wake up, work straight until dinner time, then bring their work into the bedroom at night.

While no one loves traffic or crowded public transportation systems, there is a psychological value to commuting that can be valuable to replicate in a virtual work environment. That's why so many renowned performance experts highly recommend following a personal morning routine each day rather than jumping straight into work.

Whether you want to start the day with coffee and breakfast, a brisk jog, or some inspiring reading, doing something for yourself each morning will help you enter the workday more clearheaded and energized. If you roll out of bed and look at your phone and computer right away, it often leads to an immediate dose of stress—work emails with problems that occurred overnight, reminders of deadlines, and more.

This is a terrible way to start your day; it's the equivalent of being swept from your bed into your office in your pajamas at 7:00 a.m. I don't know about you, but that would *not* be ideal for me.

The same goes for the end of the day. Many people who've spent most of their work life commuting to an office are likely to state that even though they didn't love the commute, the time spent driving home or on public transit allowed them to detach and unwind from work before stepping into their house. This is especially true for working parents, who sometimes struggle with a snap transition from work mode into parent mode.

Just as in the morning, we also encourage all our remote employees to take time to unwind as soon as the workday ends.

This was something I personally had to learn. I would finish hours of meetings and calls at six o'clock in the evening and immediately sit down to dinner with my wife and three kids. Those dinners can be a bit loud and chaotic, and I would quickly feel overwhelmed. I've learned to take at least twenty or thirty minutes at the end of the day to exercise, meditate, or take a short walk, and it makes a noticeable difference for my mental transition out of the workday.

Whether you want to walk the dog, listen to music, read, or even meditate, doing something simple once you stop working will help you de-stress after a long day in the virtual office. Plus, it will provide a reminder that you need to unplug for the evening.

On that note, it's also useful to keep any work devices out of your bedroom. Studies have shown that looking at a screen immediately before bed results in a delayed transition to a restful sleep and ensures less deep sleep.[2] Bringing your laptop to bed to answer a few emails before you go to sleep is likely to make you more fatigued and less alert for the next day. Ultimately, all you're doing is sacrificing your well-being and professional effectiveness just to answer messages that could—and often *should*—wait until morning. It's also worth getting into the habit of shutting down and putting away your smartphone for the night (ideally in a location outside your bedroom) at least an hour before bed to maximize your sleep quality. This is especially useful if you have email or work apps on your phone. These technological tools make it all too easy to go from scrolling through Instagram to reflexively checking your work email or Slack messages before bed.

Remember, you control your environment. If you take steps to prioritize your sleep, you'll feel better in the morning and be ready to attack the day.

Maintaining Motivation

Many employees are getting their first dose of remote work during a time of isolating social distancing, stressful economic turmoil, and, for many, inability to get childcare. It's no surprise that many of these workers quickly felt exhausted and began to worry they would not stay motivated while indefinitely working from home.

There are several facets of office life that compel us to come to the office every day, even if we aren't thrilled to be working. If we're lucky, there are people at the office who we're genuinely excited to see, and at the very least, we know our colleagues will notice if we don't show up. People are naturally social, and you may find you miss the social cues of working in an office when you no longer have them.

Many employees, whether they're feeling detached from the

organization, overwhelmed by their workload, or even burned out by the grind of working alone every day, are asking the same question: How do I keep myself going?

For some of us, the fact that we are employed, depended upon, and receiving a paycheck for our work is motivation enough. But if this doesn't apply to you, it can be useful to find different sources of encouragement.

Someone once told me that the fastest way to change a team's culture is to have everyone read the same book. One of the books that informed the basis of our culture is *Drive: The Surprising Truth about What Motivates Us*, *New York Times* best-selling author Daniel Pink's brilliant study of motivation. Pink argues that external motivators like paychecks, benefits, and manager praise aren't enough to keep many of us getting out of bed excited to work, as these are extrinsic motivators. Instead, we are driven by intrinsic motivation, stemming from our inherent desire to have things like autonomy, mastery, and purpose in our life and work.[3]

One way to tap into this type of motivation is to identify which aspects or tasks in your role you enjoy more than others, especially those to which you can apply your skills. If you find it invigorating to compile data in spreadsheets and draw meaning from the results, for example, you might consider finding a way to consolidate that work into blocks of time so you can look forward to that type of work, spending uninterrupted quality time on what you enjoy most.

Perhaps the most compelling motivator is what drives many of us at our core, consciously or unconsciously: a purpose. A purpose is like a topic sentence for your life, a clear articulation of what you have to offer to the world. Having taken time to articulate my personal purpose—*to share ideas that help people and organizations grow*—I find it to be an essential aligning element for my daily life and work in ways I might not have expected.

You don't have to have a clear purpose statement for your own life, though it is helpful and well worth the extensive reflection required to set one for yourself. But you can give purpose to your work by tying what you do to something you want to achieve in life. Perhaps you work for an organization whose mission you want to advance, even if your work is occasionally uninteresting. Maybe you want to acquire or develop certain skills that will help you achieve professional goals like launching a business, leading a team, or becoming an expert in your field. Or maybe you want to build a life full of travel and family, and you need a stable professional life to give you the opportunity for that level of work-life integration. Many of us actually fulfill our purpose through *how* we do something rather than *what* we are doing. Viewing purpose through this lens can take the pressure off finding your passion or the perfect job. For example, if you are someone who loves to give back, you might be better served leading that initiative for your company than working at a nonprofit.

Whatever you do for work or want in life, motivation is easier to come by if you can somehow tie the two together. Next time you are feeling unmotivated at work, spend a few minutes thinking about or writing down things that are important to you in life or goals you want to accomplish. Just the process of putting your work in the context of your broader life journey can make a noticeable difference and highlight how you can connect to those principles in new ways in your role.

Staying Focused

While remote employees aren't more likely to slack off from work and are often compelled to work more, these employees face distractions that are unique to working from home.

While you don't have to worry about what your colleagues are doing around you, you definitely have things in your home that can distract you.

If you've never worked from home before, you might expect things like the television or your smartphone to be what pull you away from work, but that's only the beginning. What can also distract you when working remotely is the realization that you still haven't washed the dishes from breakfast that morning, or that it's been a while since you took out the trash, or your carpet looks like it needs to be vacuumed. Housework that you'd neglect after a day at the office is harder to avoid when you're home all day.

You probably have an idea in mind for how naturally capable you are of focusing while working. While some people are more comfortable with long stretches of uninterrupted work and more able to ignore these types of distractions, focusing is a skill we can all practice. In fact, getting good at this skill can help us accomplish more and reduce stress.

One thing you can do to improve your focus during the workday is to prevent the distractions mentioned above. If you commit to spending a few minutes each day keeping your workspace clean and tidy and dedicate blocks of time during the day to things like doing the dishes or vacuuming your floors, you won't feel those tasks pulling you away from work. This ties back into the importance of setting a schedule. If you know you'll need to do these tasks during the day to feel more comfortable in your home office, set yourself a time to do them.

Another way to improve your focus is to practice it intentionally. One approach is a technique Cal Newport shares in his aforementioned *New York Times* bestseller, *Deep Work*. Newport recommends setting a timer for yourself, first for a short duration of time like fifteen to twenty minutes, then committing to spending that period focusing intently on a single task, such as compiling data or writing a report. If you do this, Newport says, you will become capable of focusing for gradually longer periods of time.

Now, you don't need to spend an entire eight-hour workday in an unbroken state of focus. But having the ability to shut out distractions when you need to is a valuable skill and one that you can build with time and effort. The more you can focus, the more you will accomplish and the easier it will be to unplug at the end of the workday.

Self-Care

As part of your working week, it's also essential to prioritize your health and well-being. Making time in your schedule for quality sleep and exercise won't just make you healthier, it will also improve the quality of your work. In my experience, people who barely sleep, who deal with constant stress and discord in their personal lives and pay no attention to their physical health, don't show up to work full of energy.

No matter how effectively you separate your personal and professional lives—including creating firm buffers between the two spheres—you are the same person in both areas of life; there will always be spillover.

When you're struggling with stress at work, it's often just a matter of time before that stress impacts your energy outside work, your relationships with family and friends, and your overall happiness. Likewise, if you are struggling outside work, that will eventually lead to noticeable erosion of your performance during the workday.

This can become a vicious cycle quickly, especially for remote employees, who work and live in the same space and can occasionally feel unable to fully disconnect from their jobs. Work stress leads to personal dissatisfaction, which leads to more work stress, and so on. The best way to prevent this type of spiral from happening is to take proactive steps to prioritize your self-care, both during the workday and beyond it.

To begin, it's crucial to prioritize high-quality sleep. While some people struggle more with sleep than others, there are steps anyone can take to combat these problems. One easy step is to form a consistent bedtime routine. For one week, try setting a bedtime for yourself and sticking to it. An hour before that bedtime, put away your phone, laptop, and other personal electronics, and try reading a relaxing book for thirty to sixty minutes.

While this will feel like an adjustment, before long, you'll notice that it will be easier to fall asleep at night, and you will be more rested when you wake up.

Setting a bedtime routine is especially important when

working remotely. It's far too easy to get pulled into work late at night and not detach until it's well past your ideal bedtime. Working until 2:00 a.m. only to start again at 7:00 a.m. may seem like a way to show your commitment to your job in the short term, but all it will do in the long run is burn you out and diminish your contribution at work as well.

You may also find it helpful to try incorporating consistent daily exercise into your routine and schedule. You don't need to train for a marathon or lift weights every day, but even doing a short yoga video once a day, going for a brisk walk during your lunch break, or doing a few jumping jacks before your morning coffee leads to an endorphin release that can help improve your mood and mental focus.

Finally, it's vital to find an outlet that helps you reduce your stress levels. It's important to recognize when you're feeling stressed and know what activities can help you relax and refocus.

One of our employees once shared that he occasionally catches himself in a stressed state while working. Specifically, he'll realize he's firmly clenching his jaw and drastically hunching over his computer. When he does this, he makes a concerted effort to sit back in his chair, close his eyes, and take deep, slow breaths for thirty seconds. That tiny investment of time quickly reduces tension and allows him to get back into work with a refreshed, focused mind.

There's no single activity that is best. What's most helpful is to find out what works for you. You may choose to take short meditation breaks, get up and pace around your home office, or even do some planks or burpees to get the blood flowing. While these short activities won't completely change your cumulative stress level immediately, doing them consistently will reduce your tension throughout the working week and over time.

Finally, it's useful to engage with colleagues about self-care. Reach out to someone on your team and offer to be their accountability partner, a person they can go to when they need to vent or want to brainstorm ideas for better self-care. If you enjoy yoga, running, or another specific exercise activity, reach out to your like-minded coworkers to share best practices for fitting it into the workday.

You may even consider spearheading a friendly wellness contest in your organization, working with colleagues to hold one another accountable. Many organizations have started these kinds of company-wide wellness initiatives, and if your organization hasn't done this, you can try starting one yourself.

These types of challenges don't need to have complicated rules or stringent tracking. They can just be something simple and engaging, like this example.

COMPANY WELL-BEING CHALLENGE

→ Starts October 1—sign up here.

→ Teams of six will be selected, mixing teams, regions, etc.

→ Each day, each participant must submit evidence of at least thirty minutes of doing something to benefit well-being. Fitbit photo, picture of you meditating, photo from a walk in the woods, etc.

→ For each day that each participant submits, they get one point, so a team can get up to thirty points for a week (six people over five days).

→ Ends October 31. Winners announced November 5.

Remote Reflections: Breaking Free

Imagine going from biking to work in the snow to working in a beautiful coworking space on a small Thai island. All Ben Jolly needed to do was join a remote organization to make that transformation a reality.

Jolly was an account manager on our client services team. Since ditching the office in exchange for remote work, he has lived and worked in twelve different cities, including in countries such as Mexico, Japan, Turkey, Spain, Singapore, and Thailand. Not bad for someone who dealt with crushing traffic and winter weather on his daily commute during his most recent office job.

"The main problem with working in an office for me was the commute," Jolly recalled. "I lived in Boston, and it was a struggle to get even three or four miles into the office. The public transit was bad, the weather was bad, and I was biking, but I would be biking through traffic in the snow and the rain. The commute was just miserable."

Getting rid of the commute was a huge benefit for Jolly, but it was only the beginning.

Jolly has always loved travel, but the globe-trotting possibilities that remote work offers were not on his radar before he actually started working from home. In fact, when Jolly joined our team, he had never worked virtually before and didn't even realize we were a remote organization when he sent in his application initially. But he took the opportunity to redesign his life through remote work within months of coming on board.

Jolly viewed virtual work as an escape hatch out of his home in Boston, an expensive, traffic-laden American city known for its cold winters. When his lease expired six months after he started working from home, Jolly immediately relocated.

Jolly is an example of a specific type of remote employee. Often referred to as digital nomads, these workers use the flexibility of virtual work to travel the world, immerse themselves in new cultures, learn new languages, and rack up once-in-a-lifetime experiences, all while holding full-time employment with high-quality organizations. By communicating clearly with managers and planning trips carefully, Jolly was able to live in a dozen different places for as little as a few months at a time.

Maintaining a full-time role while traveling constantly isn't necessarily easy, but Jolly found creative ways to establish normal work routines and productive habits, including conducting research before jumping to a new home. One benefit of the growing popularity of remote work in recent years and the ensuing expansion of the digital nomad community is that workers can find plenty of online resources to help them move from place to place without disrupting their professional pursuits.

Jolly carefully scouted potential landing spots, researching coworking spaces in the cities he wanted to visit to ensure he could work outside his temporary home with some frequency. He was diligent about securing high-speed internet at every new destination, including asking hosts of his targeted Airbnb to conduct speed tests on their wireless networks to ensure they had the connection speed Jolly needed to be able to work at a high level.

Like many remote employees, Jolly didn't allow his virtual work situation to affect the quality of his output. He took careful steps to ensure he could deliver a high standard of work for both clients and colleagues wherever in the world he was.

At times, this dedication even extended to working unusual

hours to match the time zone of his immediate team and client contacts. For example, while working in Istanbul, Jolly worked from 5:00 p.m. to 1:00 a.m. local time to match business hours in the eastern United States, where his clients were based. "I would always be the last one at the coworking space," Jolly said. "And in that city, you had to work in a coworking space, because home internet just wasn't consistent enough."

Jolly's story illustrates the full potential of remote work. Many virtual employees have found that if they are able to put in the effort to provide excellent professional outcomes and navigate the logistics of working from all over the world, the possibilities are nearly limitless.

Working remotely has transformed Jolly's life in more ways than one. He even met his wife while working virtually from Mexico in 2016, and she has joined him on his international journey ever since. They spent the last several years living in Asia before settling most recently in Mexico City.

It was during his time in Asia that Jolly had his most unique remote work experience.

"There's an island in Thailand called Koh Lanta, and they've really built up a remote work community there," Jolly said. "You see digital nomad 'party' communities in Asia a lot, but this one is less focused on partying and is more integrated with the local community."

Jolly spent his time at Koh Lanta working in a beautiful coworking space with a social community of like-minded virtual workers. While some international digital nomad workspaces are more isolated from their communities, Jolly was fully immersed in the local culture.

Jolly has truly become a global citizen through his travels. He has lived in many countries, learned multiple languages, and, as an avid cook, learned to prepare a wide variety of cuisines. Along the way, he has picked up ways to improve his work as well.

It's common for remote employees to need some time to develop ideal habits while working from home. It can be hard to unplug at the end of the day or to establish regular structure that allows you to feel comfortable working in an unusual environment. Because Jolly changed locations so often, developing best practices was even more important for him.

Like many other virtual workers, Jolly has found it useful to intentionally set a schedule, create a separate workspace, and develop buffer activities to demarcate the end of the workday. Jolly particularly enjoys going to coworking spaces because they help him separate his work life from his home life. To facilitate an end to his workday, he likes to cook dinner immediately after work or go to a nearby restaurant with his wife when he's able.

Jolly knows remote work isn't for everyone, but he notes

that people working from home for the first time during the pandemic aren't getting the ideal virtual work experience. Things like dodging difficult commutes and traveling more easily will be much more appealing after life returns to normal. Likewise, the experience will feel less isolating when virtual workers are allowed to resume their preferred social activities beyond the workday.

Regardless, there is no question for Jolly that the benefits of working from home clearly outweigh any possible drawbacks.

"Remote work has been amazing," Jolly said. "I never thought I would see this much of the world or experience this much. I have no complaints."

Building Social Connections

A concern that some people have when transitioning to remote work is the fear of feeling isolated. While working in an office means dealing with coworkers who may talk too loudly on the phone or take up your space at a communal worktable, working from home deprives you of typical in-office benefits like group lunches or spontaneous drop-ins or happy hours.

Like many other aspects of remote work, it's possible to address this concern with planning and follow-through. It's helpful to remember that when you're on a virtual team, your colleagues are also working from home and are often interested in building personal connections with coworkers.

Many of these connections can be built on a one-on-one basis. It's common in remote organizations for colleagues to arrange short, social catch-up calls where they join a video call and talk about nonwork topics for twenty to thirty minutes. Coworkers can arrange virtual lunches or coffee breaks during the day or meet for a virtual happy hour at the end of the day to relax and bond.

As with many facets of remote work, the situation is often what you make of it. You may go beyond these basic ideas and set up social group chats or discussion boards in whatever communications platform your team uses. You can start a book club and even select books focused on personal development to help one another grow.

Finally, although the pandemic has made this more difficult, remote employees can still gather in person. Many organizations hire multiple employees in a given geographic area, so you may be just a short drive away from your nearest colleague. Meeting with a colleague to spend a day or even a few hours at a coffee shop or coworking space can help you stay connected.

Extroverts and Introverts

While there are several best practices that can help you adapt, there isn't a one-size-fits-all approach to remote work, as most people are wired very differently. It can be useful to better understand some of your core personality traits and to delve into one core personality difference in particular, as it's especially relevant to remote work: the difference between introversion and extroversion.

First, it's useful to set a simple definition of each of these categories. Extroverts prefer high-energy environments, consistently surrounding themselves with many other people. In contrast, introverts prefer lower-stimulation environments, enjoy quiet concentration, or even take a more cautious approach to risk. While introverts enjoy spending time with others, they're more comfortable doing so in smaller groups and calmer environments.

Remote work, especially during the isolation of a pandemic, has often been framed as an extrovert's nightmare and an introvert's dream. It's true that introverts, who get energy from working quietly by themselves, are perhaps more likely to adapt quickly to working from home. But both extroverts and introverts have advantages and challenges to tackle in the virtual workplace and have adjustments they can make to better excel.

For extroverts, the challenge of remote work is obvious:

instead of being surrounded by people to interact with when they need a shot of energy, they are at home and often isolated. Before long, working in silence becomes draining.

The best way extroverts can tackle this is by proactively creating opportunities to recharge in a social environment. This is easier outside a pandemic, when you can schedule lunch with a friend, go to a crowded cafe to work with some background noise, or fill evenings with happy hours, dinners with friends, and other social engagements.

In pandemic times, there are still steps extroverts can take to get a boost. Consider arranging evening video calls with friends or safely distanced outdoor activities with others. At work, you can reach out to other extroverts on your team and ask to set up a standing virtual lunch or coffee time, just to have the chance to talk to another person with some regularity during the working week.

Extroverts are probably jealous of their introverted colleagues, for whom remote work is an escape from an overstimulating office environment. However, introverts must similarly overcome some of their tendencies to thrive in a virtual workplace.

First, video calls are perhaps more difficult than in-person meetings for everyone to have a chance to speak up equally. You have likely been on a video conference where two employees spoke at once, only for the quieter one to cede the floor to their colleague. Introverts can be overstimulated by these types of meetings as is, especially given that a camera is constantly on them, and they may decide it's easiest to stay silent until the call is over when they can have time to properly reflect and process the information in their preferred low-stimulation work environment.

This can extend beyond meetings as well. Introverts might be less willing to reach out to colleagues with questions or ideas so as not to disturb them. They may be less inclined to join virtual company social events without having extroverts in the office to encourage them to join. If you've worked in an office, you have probably seen more outgoing colleagues making the rounds and encouraging more reserved employees to join them on their way to happy hour with the rest of the team. This is, of course, less likely to happen in a virtual environment.

Just as extroverts must proactively plan to feed their need for socialization while working remotely, introverts need to occasionally push themselves to speak up in a virtual setting. Even small steps such as committing to ask a question in every meeting or to speak a certain number of times can make a difference.

It's important for managers to understand this difference as well. Just as many teachers choose not to call on the students who are eager to share and constantly have their hand up, managers should recognize that some of their employees are less inclined to speak up in meetings or participate in team social activities, and some thoughtful encouragement can make a difference in that employee's engagement and development.

Even if you aren't a manager, it can be helpful to be mindful of your introverted and extroverted colleagues and take opportunities to make their experiences better. You can make a difference in someone's workday by inviting your outgoing colleague to a virtual coffee or by helping your quieter coworker speak up if it's clear they have something to say.

When to Use Video

Our company, like many others, makes a point of using video calls as much as possible, both internally within a team and externally with clients. Video calls are more effective at building trust and having clear communications than just talking on the phone. If meeting in person is a ten out of ten, I like to say speaking on the phone is a four and video calls are a seven or eight.

Not everyone is comfortable with video calls yet, even though COVID-19 forced many people to embrace the format for the first time. I remember I once did a video call with a client, and when they realized their video was showing on Zoom, they ducked under the desk. No joke, they dove out of view. It was just not something they had done before in that context. And that's their choice.

But even if our clients or sales prospects don't want to show their video, we leave ours on anyway. We believe it builds rapport and creates more engagement, and we saw most of the businesses we work with adopting a similar approach during the pandemic.

It's much easier to tell on video if people are paying attention, and their facial expressions are often revealing. Once, I was on a sales call where one of our team members was in a car, not using video. They rambled for too long, and I could see in the prospect's video feed that they lost interest in the pitch. The salesperson, who wasn't using video, had no idea, so they weren't able to adjust in real time.

With that said, it's important to recognize that video calls create more fatigue than in-person or phone meetings; this is why you've probably heard the term *Zoom fatigue*. There are a number of scientific reasons for this; for starters, many video conference users feel the need to make constant, unbroken eye contact with their screens—or the green dot of their camera—which can be exhausting over long periods of time.[4]

In addition, small pauses in a conversation, which are normal in face-to-face meetings, become stressful, as everyone on the call worries their technology has failed or quickly jumps to fill the awkward silence.[5] While video calls have been a huge advancement, there is mounting evidence that they are far more mentally taxing than in-person or phone conversations.

By now, millions of workers know the feeling of spending four straight hours on video calls, feeling the mental strain of needing to appear completely focused and engaged the entire time. Most of us don't enjoy staring in a mirror for hours at a time, and seeing ourselves on screen for long periods can be similarly disorienting. One way to mitigate this is to use speaker view, especially on one-on-one calls, so the screen of the person speaking is larger and easier to focus on.

We used to require video calls whenever possible, but as virtual meetings have become more common, we've come to recognize the cumulative impact of video fatigue, which seems to be reached after three to five hours of video calls. Because so many formerly in-person meetings are now on video, a helpful adjustment is to shift more internal calls, where there is already a good working relationship, to your mobile phone, giving you the option to sit outside, go for a walk around the neighborhood, or even pace around your home to get the blood flowing while you talk.

To recap, here are some great tips for managing remote video calls:

▸ Reserve video calls for external meetings, brainstorming

sessions, all-company meetings, or internal calls about sensitive topics, such as delivering employee feedback.

▶ Use the phone for informal meetings with colleagues, fifteen-minute check-ins, or group calls where you are just listening in and don't need to participate.

Leveraging Asynchronous Video

There is another great way to use video for one-way communications, with a method that is becoming a lot more popular: asynchronous, or one-way, video.

It's increasingly common for global companies to have employees in widely distributed time zones, and it can be difficult to gather all those employees on the same call. When delivering a company-wide message, asking our 170+ people to join a call is less efficient than sending everybody a video message and asking them to watch it at their convenience. It can also be much more personal than a long email and faster to create, and it better conveys the proper emotions. Platforms like Zoom, Loom, BombBomb, and Vidyard are perfect for recording these types of videos.

Not only does asynchronous video work well for team or all-company messages, it's also increasingly useful for individual communications. For example, if you receive an email that requires a thoughtful or careful reply, it can save a lot of time to record a quick video response rather than crafting and editing a detailed written reply. So instead of spending an hour writing and editing a complex email, you can record a video replying to the person in less than five minutes and capture the conversational style of an in-person discussion in the process. One of our leadership team members shifted her written end-of-month updates to asynchronous video during the pandemic and probably won't be going back to what she did before, as she enjoys having one less thing to write.

Written communication isn't second nature for many people. In a remote environment, it's easy for a person to write an unclear message regarding an important issue, then have team members misinterpret the meaning or course of action from it. Asynchronous video avoids this by allowing the sender to articulate exactly what they need to say and include important cues such as tone of voice and body language.

Asynchronous video can also help keep employees' schedules more open. If an employee or colleague asks a question that's difficult to answer over email, you don't have to schedule a meeting to share your response. You can just record a video, send it, and trust that the message is received with the appropriate context.

As with most professional communications, it's important

to know when to use asynchronous video. Because the recipient doesn't have the opportunity to respond in real time, it's not ideal for sensitive topics such as conflict resolution, critical feedback, or other potentially contentious situations. It should never be used for performance management. However, it's well suited for informational downloads such as explaining a process, updating a group, delivering a training, or briefing a colleague on the status of a project.

It can seem unnatural, especially in some professional cultures, to receive a message where a person is talking at you without having the opportunity to respond. It's important for employees to know this when preparing an asynchronous video, to tell the recipient what the video will include in advance, and to give a clear avenue the recipient can use to respond with their questions and comments for further discussion if necessary.

Relocation

One of the enticing qualities of working remotely is the possibility of relocating. While some remote workers will only want to move a bit farther from the center of their home city, others may take the opportunity to move to a different state or country without the burden of finding a new job.

Many organizations allow employees to do this, but it's

important to consider some key questions before putting your house on the market or getting out of your apartment lease.

First, you should determine where you are actually allowed to move to. If you're relocating to a state or country where your organization doesn't already have employees, you shouldn't assume your employer will agree to let you go there and remain with the company. Different countries and states have different work regulations, tax laws, and benefit requirements, and there may be some places where it's just too onerous or expensive to allow employees to live. This is not something you want to have come to light after you've already signed a lease or moved.

While it's probably easier to get approval to move to a state, country, or region where your company already has workers, especially if they have a cluster of employees there, don't assume that is the case. Proactively approach your HR representative, tell them what you are considering, and ask whether it's feasible and if it will result in any changes to your pay, benefits, etc. For example, depending on your organization's policy, it is possible your pay will be affected by a relocation. Organizations tend to consider their market's cost of living when they set employee compensation. If you move to a significantly cheaper area, your company may want to renegotiate compensation accordingly. In fact, this is already occurring. Some large tech companies have announced that they will decrease compensation for employees who move away from expensive cities such as San Francisco, New York, and London, where higher pay is necessary to account for a high cost of living.[6]

Moving also has tax and benefit implications to consider. If you receive healthcare coverage through your employer, you may need to enroll in a different healthcare plan when you relocate, even to a different state, as many insurance providers don't offer coverage nationwide. Different states, regions, and countries also have widely variant tax laws, so it's important to know in advance what taxes you'll be subject to in your potential new home.

For example, while some countries and states tax you based on where you live and work, others may go by where the company has an office or headquarters. This may significantly reduce the value of moving to an area with more favorable tax laws.

Having the flexibility to live where you want is a significant draw of remote work, but it's important to do your research before you commit to a move.

Broadening Work-Life Horizons

Most of us can still remember counting down the final days of school and eagerly anticipating the freedom of summer vacation.

Miranda Barrett is years removed from school, but she still

gets that feeling every summer—when there isn't a global pandemic, that is.

Barrett has been a fully remote worker since 2017, first as a consultant and most recently as vice president of member success at the U.S.-based member association, the Community Company. Her story is perhaps the best-case scenario for designing a life around remote work.

"When you have kids and they're in school, it's not like you're bouncing around the world," Barrett, a mother of two boys, said. "The summers, however, are magical. I am able to build out a whole fun summer for us, and as long as I can work out camps and childcare, I'm able to work with consistency and availability."

In summer 2019, Barrett and her family traveled for seven weeks, visiting places like North Carolina, Vermont, and California. In a previous summer, she took her older son on an extended trip to California and Hawaii. These trips did not require vacation or time off from work. She worked during normal work hours, including leading a department of thirty-five employees, while at the same time creating lifelong memories with her kids outside her work hours.

Though the pandemic canceled Barrett's travel plans for summer 2020, her family still made a big move. Rather than social distancing in their Arlington home—a "shoebox" in Barrett's words—the family moved to a relative's farmhouse in rural Virginia, where they began raising goats, chickens, and foster dogs.

Postpandemic: The Future for Remote Workers

While many experiencing remote work realities for the first time in 2020 did not have the chance to recreate Barrett's experience, her story illustrates the possibilities that remote work holds beyond the pandemic.

In considering the future of remote work, it is worth noting that COVID-19 has forced virtual employees to work under conditions and constraints that would be abnormal or even inappropriate in usual circumstances. If you are working remotely for the first time under these pandemic conditions, it's important to consider that future remote work opportunities you may have will be different and much easier.

Employees who continue working remotely after the rest of their lifestyle returns to normal will likely find virtual work to be easier and more fulfilling under less extreme conditions. These are some crucial differences that remote work will hold after the pandemic finally passes.

First, as emphasized earlier, working parents won't have their kids homeschooling in the background and will be expected to arrange childcare during the workday once it is safe to do so.

Employees will be increasingly expected to have a more formal office setup—a specific part of their home designated for work, better lighting, appropriate technology, a clean background, and other professional touches. While creating these will require some logistical coordination, it'll also make remote work feel more comfortable and normal. You'll feel like you're working from home, not living at work.

Remote work will feel less isolating when employees can use their flexibility to go to a class at the gym during the day, grocery shop on their lunch break, or see friends for coffee or an after-work happy hour. As Barrett's experiences show, it's even common for remote employees to travel, using their flexibility to work from a different or new location that they can explore during their free time. These types of arrangements must be carefully planned and agreed upon with managers, but they'd be simply impossible for office-only workers.

On a higher level, remote work offers an opportunity for people to expand their lifestyle options and have a real choice on where and how they want to live. While many people around the world live in cities because they truly want to, many do so because they need to be close to the best opportunities in their industry. For decades, employees have needed to endure increasingly longer commutes in order to obtain a balance of the career they wanted and the space they needed personally at a price they could afford.

In a world where remote work is available at many organizations, people can truly choose where they want to live. People who want to live in the suburbs to raise a family can seek out a remote organization, allowing them to design the personal lifestyle they want without professional trade-offs.

Couples won't need to deal with the strain of one person following their partner's work opportunity to another city and having to leave their own career behind. Traffic for the employees who choose to commute will decrease, and public transit will be less crowded.

Ask yourself—if you could live anywhere, with no professional constraints, would you choose to live where you live now? Would you prefer to live farther from a city center in exchange for a larger home with a better home office? Whatever your answer may be, working remotely offers a different world of possibilities for you.

All told, it's likely that remote workers will find it easier to work from home when the pandemic finally passes. People who are on the fence about virtual work during the pandemic may find themselves far happier and more comfortable under normal conditions. And people who like remote work now will likely enjoy it even more!

This is the new frontier for work-life integration. Working remotely will give people the opportunity to decide how they want to integrate work with their preferred lifestyle rather than needing to live in a certain place based on the career opportunities available.

With that said, remote work is not for everyone, nor for the demands of their job. Barrett's husband, a reporter for the *Washington Post*, is counting the days until he can return to the newsroom. But having worked remotely for years and managed several virtual employees, she's convinced many people who try it will never want to return to the office.

"There's really just no limit to what you can do with it," Barrett said. "I don't know what the future holds for us, as far as where we'll live and what we'll do, but I am not willing to give up the level of flexibility I have with remote working."

PART TWO

Thriving
as a Remote
Organization

3

It Starts with Culture

Employees have significant control over their own remote work experience. The way they schedule their day, set up their home office, and manage their energy is a crucial part of a healthy, productive virtual career. But organizational leaders have an even bigger role to play in making remote work effective in their organization.

If you're committed to making your organization remote and want to excel over the long haul, it's crucial to lay the proper cultural foundation to ensure your employees are put in the best possible position to succeed, and that culture may need to look different from the one you have today. Giving your team a list of best practices and procedures is helpful, but it's even more important to take a close look at your organization's principles, operating systems, and infrastructure to ensure your remote culture is both healthy and high-performing.

As with all things in business, the day-to-day operations of a team depend on the cultural foundation set by the company's leadership. So we'll start by addressing these foundational elements of a healthy, high-performing remote culture, then dig more into the system that supports that culture.

It's worth noting that I wasn't always passionate about culture. Candidly, I used to believe many publicized company cultures were phony and the concept of mission, vision, and core values was bullshit to keep a legion of consultants busy coming up with clever office wall art.

For years, I would walk into corporate offices and see walls plastered with generic core values like "Honesty" and "Teamwork" and "Integrity." Not only did these platitudes sound like something any company could state, but I had also seen these same companies with idealistic core values flagrantly violate those same principles consistently with their actions.

United Airlines is a pertinent example of this problem. United's core values statement says, "fly right, fly friendly, fly together, and fly above and beyond." Their culture is supposedly built on "connecting people and uniting the world."

That made it especially galling when, in April 2017, United caused a huge controversy when one of their passengers was dragged off an overbooked flight by airport security. After making the decision to oversell the flight, United declined to offer a large-enough financial incentive to compel any customers to give up their seats voluntarily on the plane. Instead, they resorted to brute force, literally dragging a battered and bloodied David Dao off the aircraft, a scene that was filmed by other passengers and made its way around the internet in no time. The backlash was immediate.

By trying to avoid the cost of a few hundred dollars in compensation to customers who had done nothing wrong, United created a controversy that lost the company an estimated $800 million in market capitalization. While United's culture was ostensibly built on uniting and connecting the world, what they actually did was unite the public *against them.*

There are plenty of examples like this in business, and seeing many of these cases left me feeling cynical about culture, even as it could apply to our own company. Seeing companies promote generic, PR-friendly principles but not observing that behavior in the people at their organization felt like a jarring disconnect that rightly made employees dubious about these practices and the concept of company culture overall.

Ironically, it was another airline that shifted my thinking on culture. Herb Kelleher, founder of Southwest Airlines, was always one of my business idols. Kelleher built an upstart low-cost airline into the most respected and profitable airline business in the United States, and he did so by embracing unconventional thinking and out-innovating far bigger competitors.

At a conference I attended in 2013, I saw a speaker who'd had the chance to interview Kelleher about Southwest's formula for success. The speaker revealed that when he asked Kelleher how, from 1990 to 2000, Southwest had made more profit than the entire U.S. airline industry, Kelleher simply replied with one word: *culture*.

I was expecting Kelleher to attribute Southwest's success to their frugalness and efficiency, their anti-hub strategy, their clever marketing, or their legendary humor and customer service. Hearing that answer made me completely rethink my stance on organizational culture, and I started to do some research.

If you examine Southwest's culture doctrine, you'll notice something very different from other companies. Here's how they define their core values:

LIVE THE SOUTHWEST WAY

- Warrior Spirit
- Servant's Heart
- Fun-LUVing Attitude [sic]

WORK THE SOUTHWEST WAY

▶ Work Safely

▶ Wow Our Customers

▶ Keep Costs Low

Rather than using cookie-cutter value statements, Southwest's core values represent a differentiated point of view that's unique to their organization and ties into many of the things they do well. More importantly, their values are clearly visible in the business's daily operations. The question remains—does Southwest Airlines really demonstrate these values in practice, or are they just lip service? The following story helps answer that question.

In 2015, Peggy Uhle boarded a Southwest flight in Chicago, the second leg in her trip from Raleigh-Durham to Columbus, Ohio. As the plane was taxiing to the runway, it suddenly turned around and returned to the gate. The crew then called Uhle's name over the intercom and asked her to exit the plane.

When Uhle reached the terminal, Southwest employees informed her that her son had been in a terrible accident in Denver and was in a coma. After delivering the devastating news, Southwest employees led Uhle to a private room, proactively booked her on the next flight to Denver, ensured she was the first person on and off the plane, and even packed a free meal for her. Southwest then routed Uhle's luggage to the hospital in Denver and ordered a car to pick her up from the airport.

Southwest doesn't have an operating manual for a situation as specific and sensitive as Uhle's, but they have a clear, specific culture and values that include "wow our customers" and show a "servant's heart." The employees knew what to do based on Southwest's unique, reinforced values. They didn't have to escalate to an executive for permission; they just sprang into action and went above and beyond for a customer in a time of need and got a great outcome that was shared widely in the press, eliciting a very different reaction from United's actions.

Southwest presents the best possible outcome when an organization's culture manifests itself. Employees know what to do even when leadership isn't watching. They know what the company's values are, and they know how to live them and make them actionable. This type of mentality is particularly important in remote environments—when your employees work under limited supervision and need to make key decisions in pivotal moments.

The sudden shift to remote work that several organizations made during the pandemic underscored a key fact about organizational culture: your culture should not be dependent on in-person connections or frequent meetings and events. It's essential to build a culture based on nonnegotiable principles, objectives, and operating standards that employees can follow whether they're in an office or their own homes.

Cultural Overhaul

Culture isn't just what's formed when a company starts. While Kelleher is a great example of how a founder can impact the DNA of an organization for decades, culture can also be the force that transforms organizations of any size or global reach. Organizations facing a transformative moment, such as a pandemic or a global shift toward remote work, can and should make their culture the focal point of that change.

Garry Ridge, CEO of the WD-40 Company, is an example of someone who created a significant cultural change at a company that was already iconic in many ways.

WD-40 has been a globally recognizable brand for decades. If you've seen it before, you can probably picture their distinctive blue and yellow can with a red top. But despite selling a popular product and building a global reach, the company had plenty of places to improve when Ridge was promoted to CEO in 1997.

While WD-40 was quite successful when Ridge took the reins, the organization had an employee engagement rate of just 40 percent. That engagement deficit was defined by a lack of trust and transparency.

Since taking over, Ridge has grown the company's value from $300 million to $2.4 billion over the course of his tenure and improved WD-40's employee engagement to 93 percent, despite leading a globally dispersed team of five hundred employees.

Just like Kelleher, Ridge insists that all company results stem from establishing and reinforcing the right cultural principles.

"You can't get results optimized without culture. And one of the challenges is that organizations spend a balance of time between strategy and execution, versus people, purpose, and values," Ridge said. "I think we've proven over time that certainly strategy and execution are ultimately important. But if you want to turbocharge your strategy, and in particular your execution, you need to have highly engaged people."

As Ridge tells it, knowledge was power within the organization in the years before he took over, causing employees to rarely share their best practices or tactics with others, because their value was in their singular expertise. Similarly, employees were afraid to ask for help or to take bold action because fear of failure was pervasive throughout the organization. On a global team, sharing is necessary to ensure the entire organization follows best practices, communicates clearly, and is dedicated to helping the team grow. But WD-40 employees worked according to a troubling unspoken mantra: every man and woman for themselves.[1]

Ridge understood that WD-40 needed a cultural overhaul, but he also recognized that many immediate, systemic changes to a global organization would be onerous to communicate and install. Instead, he started by making one major change that redefined the company's culture in a productive way: a consistent prioritization of learning.

"We take every situation and look at it as a learning opportunity. So we took the word 'failure' out and replaced it with 'the learning moment,'" Ridge said. "And that really opened people up into a safety zone of being able to share without fear of embarrassment, ridicule, or whatever. And that's been a huge part of the change in our culture."

That single change didn't transform WD-40's culture by itself, but it was the galvanizing moment for a massive shift in the organization's cultural foundation. It became clear to employees that the company's leadership was most concerned with creating an environment of consistent, proactive learning and that failure and struggle in pursuit of learning were encouraged. Employees suddenly felt empowered to learn and view mistakes as lessons, and they were taught to share information readily and teach their colleagues rather than keeping their expertise close to the vest to maximize their value to the organization.

With a collective commitment to learning as the impetus, Ridge gradually remade WD-40's entire culture into one built on shared identity, trust, and compassion. The company does not see itself as a seller of industrial lubricants. Instead, its mission is "To create positive lasting memories in everything we do." The WD-40 family of products is about helping customers make memories.

Today, WD-40 refers to its employees as a tribe, and the company has a commitment to making life and work enjoyable for its colleagues. Ridge's team is dedicated to building close, mutually beneficial relationships with both customers and coworkers. The company also creates an unwavering culture of accountability for all employees, especially its leaders.

That last point may be the most important. Leaders and managers must understand their roles in setting the bar high for employees and coaching them to meet it. While a certain standard of commitment and effort is required of employees in world-class organizations, companies with healthy, high-performing cultures have leaders who recognize that they are responsible for the team's performance. Managers at WD-40, whom Ridge refers to as coaches, consider it their job to lead employees to top performance.

"If we've done our job, if we've clearly identified and agreed with our tribe member what an A performance looks like, the responsibility of helping that person get that A is the coach's," Ridge said.

Ridge asks each leader in his organization to teach and lead others by looking in the mirror. Organizations with poor culture and poor outcomes, which often manage by blame and fear, tend to be that way because leaders are either not interested in helping employees thrive or not capable of it. These are the organizations where employees are afraid to give feedback, work eighty-hour weeks in hopes of proving their worth, and face either demotivating micromanagement or apathy from key leadership. All these factors become far more problematic in a remote environment.

It's easy to see why it's necessary to define culture broadly before we dig into the particulars of creating a healthy and engaged remote organization. The core foundations of top cultures such as WD-40 are fundamental to a top-performing remote organization. People need to be unafraid to take initiative and work without supervision. They need to be encouraged to share information and best practices openly with their colleagues. They need to feel like they're part of a team, where their work is part of something bigger and more important, and that they have the support of their colleagues across the organization.

If you are attempting to transition your company to a virtual workplace, you are going to need to take a hard look at your culture and determine whether it is the right foundation to build on. There may be issues lying dormant in your company's processes, communication methods, and even vision and values that will become very evident without the benefit of an office to bring your team together each day.

Let's start by defining company culture and the core elements that form its foundation.

Defining Culture

Now we reach a key question: what is culture? After extensive reflection and research, I came to a two-pronged definition. Culture is (1) your organization's operating system and (2) how people make decisions when you're not in the room.

Building a world-class culture requires authentic leadership. An organization's leaders must have self-awareness; they need to possess knowledge of who they are and what they value most. To build a great culture that you can effectively lead, it's important to draw inspiration from your own personal principles and priorities. I don't believe you can build a lasting culture that's not a reflection of your own personal values in some way, because if it isn't, you won't be able to authentically lead it.

In exploring and developing my understanding of great organizational cultures, I've had the opportunity to work with hundreds of organizations and study high-performing companies across all categories: business, nonprofit, civic, and otherwise.

And I've continually found the same five principles in these organizations, which I call the Mighty Five:

- ▸ Vision
- ▸ Values
- ▸ Goals
- ▸ Consistency
- ▸ Clarity

The first three are core components, and the last two are modifiers that dictate the execution of those components.

First, successful companies have clear, forward-thinking **vision**. They have a clear picture and story about where they're going, and they can articulate that vision in a way that excites their stakeholders, both internally and externally.

An organization works to achieve its vision in the service of its **values**, the nonnegotiable principles that dictate how the company and its employees should operate. This is where the Southwest example is salient—they became profitable by operating according to their values, not by treating customers poorly and dragging them off planes.

Great cultures also have clear **goals** that build toward their vision and support their values. In the game of pursuing your vision, goals are your scoreboard. If your company hits a bunch of goals that don't connect to your vision, those goals will be empty or meaningless achievements. They won't get you where you want to go.

The modifiers to vision, values, and goals are **consistency** and **clarity**. Effective organizations have consistent vision, consistent values, and consistent goals. Employees don't worry about the company's core goals and principles changing every week or month. These organizations also have clear vision, clear values, and clear goals. Everybody understands what they are and how to follow them in their daily work.

For remote organizations, your culture cannot just be a series of buzzwords on a wall. In fact, virtual companies don't even have walls on which to display those platitudes. As you'll see in the upcoming pages, it's essential to ensure every employee can quickly identify the vision, values, and goals of the organization and understand how they can live those principles in their daily work.

You might be thinking, "How can you talk about great cultures without discussing people?" People are obviously crucial to any company's success, but you can't identify the right people until you decide what kind of company you want to build. It's putting the cart before the horse. This is particularly true of remote companies. If you try to hire your team without knowing what your principles and goals are, you may be hiring people who aren't the right fit for your organization.

In sports, general managers hire their coaches and determine strategy before they recruit players for their specific system, because a great player in one system might not adapt well to another. Great organizations are about the success of the team; they don't change their playbook or entire system for a single player.

These five attributes are the biggest factors in determining whether your organization succeeds or fails in building a great culture. Let's dig into each one in detail.

Vision

At Acceleration Partners, our vision statement is "To lead the partner marketing revolution while changing the work–life paradigm." That's the topic sentence for our organization, and people who resonate with that vision reflexively want to work with us; it means something real to them. But while a vision statement is a key component, it's helpful to go a step further to bring this to life for current and prospective employees.

For guidance on how to do this, I've drawn particular inspiration from two friends of mine, leading Canadian business thinkers Brian Scudamore and Cameron Herold. Scudamore and Herold previously worked as business partners for the global commercial junk-removal company, 1-800-GOT-JUNK?

Scudamore is the founder and CEO, and Herold was his first COO. The pair scaled the business and popularized a transformational leadership tool along the way. In 2000, with the company stagnating at $1 million in revenue, Scudamore realized he and Herold needed to create a bold vision of where the company would be three years in the future. He headed off to his cabin for a few days and created a picture of the company in 2003, which he called the Painted Picture. This included a narrative document that told the story of exactly what working in the organization would be like for the company's leadership and employees, three years hence.

Scudamore turned the Painted Picture into a one-page poster that he framed in the company's main office. The document was heavy on details, not only discussing business achievements like franchise expansion but also including more personal details such as how employees and customers would describe their experiences with the company. Scudamore even included a personal appearance on *The Oprah Winfrey Show* as part of the vision.

By 2003, the company had achieved 96 percent of the goals outlined in the vision and was on the path to exponential growth. To this day, Scudamore creates a new Painted Picture for the organization, which has now grown to over $250 million in annual revenue, every few years.[2]

And in case you're wondering, Scudamore did appear on *The Oprah Winfrey Show*, right on schedule, in 2003.

Later, as a business coach, Herold turned the practice into an exercise he called Vivid Vision. The central key to this idea is to write a present-tense narrative with a specific future date in mind, describing in detail what the company looks and feels like at that time and how people act.

Inspired by Scudamore and Herold, we decided to sit down in late 2016 and write a Vivid Vision for our company.[3] Our first edition described what our company would look and feel like on January 1, 2020.

We wrote that we were going to triple our company's revenue and build our number of employees to over one hundred. We were going to write the first book about the partner marketing industry, choosing *Performance Partnerships* as the title. We were going to win several major company culture awards that we hadn't yet received. And we were going to have a global business in four countries.

This seemed audacious at the time. We had some skeptics on our team and, I have to admit, I had my own doubts. However, we started to share it widely—with our team members, prospective employees, clients, and partners. We even shared it with our bank when we went to ask for a credit line increase, and they agreed to double our line after seeing how accurate our predictions had been. Having a vision written in such clear detail became a North Star for where we were going that we could use to attract the right people, structure our goals, and measure our progress. For people who weren't excited by where we were headed, it also gave them a chance to opt out of the journey, which was a mutually beneficial outcome.

In late 2019, we celebrated hitting nearly every single one of those goals at our annual company event. By that point, I had already sat down and spent two months writing our next Vivid Vision for what our business will look like on January 1, 2023. We have every intention of continuing the cycle from there.

Values

Core values are the DNA of a successful person at your company. You need to get this right when you hire them, because if they don't have or demonstrate that value, they won't be a match for your organization. A core value needs to be worded in a way that is objective and evaluative, so you can easily measure someone's behavior or performance against that value. Someone who meets all your core values is almost always a top performer when they are in the right role.

For example, organizational core values are the hallmark of the culture that Ridge and his team have built at WD-40.

Specifically, WD-40's values are hierarchical, which means that if there is any conflict between values in a given decision or circumstance, the higher one wins.

Here are their six values, in hierarchical order, the first being the most important:

- ▸ We value doing the right thing.
- ▸ We value creating positive, lasting memories in all our relationships.
- ▸ We value making it better than it is today.
- ▸ We value succeeding as a tribe while excelling as individuals.
- ▸ We value owning it and passionately acting on it.
- ▸ We value sustaining the WD-40 Company economy.

When discussing his employees, Ridge likes to say that any person at his company is safe making a decision under one or more of their core values. Even if mistakes—or learning moments—occur, they will be forgiven and learned from, as long as the employee was making them in service of the core values. As a leader, do you feel as secure in your core values to make the same statement?

And with core values, less is more.

When we first developed our own company core values, we had six: **Accountability**, **Figure It Out**, **Always Get Better**, **Get Stuff Done + Excellence**, **Genuine Partnership**, and **No**

Jerks. I loved our core values and thought they were perfect, but even I needed an acronym to remember them all. During the first year of a three-year entrepreneurial master's degree program, as part of a discussion on culture, a woman in our class who had an incredible company culture made an impassioned case for having only three core values. By having three simple core values, the company clarified the most important things to the business in a way that was easy to remember, understand, and apply. No mnemonic devices or acronyms were needed. She also shared that companies that have five or six values often had overlapping values that were part of the same higher-level concept.

After some thought, I realized she was right. We reassessed our core values and decided many of them were similar and could be merged. Now, we only have three: **Own It**, **Excel and Improve**, and **Embrace Relationships**. Everyone in our company should be able to tell you these three core values. We talk about them every day, our managers consistently teach and reinforce them, and they dictate how everybody throughout the organization behaves and is rewarded.

You have to invest time and effort to ensure your core values are in alignment when leading a remote organization. In a virtual environment, you need to have clear, widely understood principles that people can use to guide their actions and decision-making when they're not supervised and so you know your team is operating under the same principles.

They will also help you proactively identify which employees are a good fit for your team. If a prospective employee doesn't appear to reflect your company's values, my experience is that they rarely work out in the long term. For example, people who prefer consensus decision-making and need constant oversight might not excel in a company built on self-directed work and initiative. They are likely to be a much better fit for a different organization that values those attributes.

Again, core values are the DNA of what makes an employee successful at your organization. They're not marketing material to be shared on a wall or a flyer. They should dictate how you expect your team to behave and what behavior you reward.

Having a small number of core values makes it easier to evaluate whether employees are emulating those principles. If you have six core values, as our team used to, it's easy to think an employee hitting five out of six core values is good enough. But if your company has three core values, as we do now, if you only demonstrate two of them, that is a score of only 66 percent—not a passing grade by most standards of excellence. It's much easier to determine if a person is the right fit when you only use a few crucial criteria.

Core values should be fully integrated parts of your

organization. They should guide all key personnel decisions that management makes. They should be the most important rubric to determine how to reward, promote, and recognize employees. They should also be a crucial evaluating factor when delivering feedback to employees and helping them improve. At our company, we even present annual awards to employees who are named for each of our core values—more on that to come.

WHERE TO USE CORE VALUES

- ▶ Hiring
- ▶ Major strategic decisions/brainstorming (i.e., does this course build off our core values?)
- ▶ Performance management conversations and decisions
- ▶ Promotions and pay increases
- ▶ Recognition programs and awards
- ▶ Project debriefs
- ▶ Company communications
- ▶ Clarifying questions (i.e., did this meet our standard of **Own It?**)
- ▶ Customer or client feedback

Goals

Goals are the key metrics that allow you to hold yourself and your team accountable. Goals shouldn't just be targets that sound impressive to your team or your customers. They have to build upon each other to advance the vision and values you've carefully crafted.

Your organization's long-term vision, discussed above, should be the basis for your annual goals. Each of these yearly goals are things you need to reach to achieve the core elements of your vision by the end date. Because our Vivid Vision spans three years, our team breaks three years into twelve quarters of goals and key metrics we need to reach our targets. Then we make them public for our entire team to see.

Accountability is important in any organization, but it's particularly important in a remote one. The best way to be accountable is to put everything into a system that can be used by the entire team and provide real-time updates and progress. We currently use an online tool called Metronome Growth Systems that tracks everybody's goals, from the leadership team down, but there are plenty of other tools that do this as well. Everybody's metrics, goals, and weekly progress toward those targets are visible for the company to see, with each one assigned to a person's name with a red, yellow, or green light measuring how they are doing.

This is crucial to getting your entire team in alignment. Each of our team members can look at their own goals and metrics for the year and see how they feed into the organization's goals in that same span. It's crucial for lower-level employees to understand that their work is building toward something bigger for the organization.

Similarly, this creates accountability for senior leaders in the company as well. Executive teams shouldn't hide their goals and metrics. They should make those numbers visible to the entire organization so they can set the standard and be held accountable as well.

One of the most common questions we get about our remote culture is how do you know people are actually getting their work done at home? When the company's goals and the employee goals that support them are all laid out clearly and transparently, there's no ambiguity about what employees are expected to accomplish or why it is important.

People who consistently fall short of their goals or their stated commitments know they will be supported but held accountable. This becomes another great mechanism of self-selection around our primary core value of **Own It**. People who are motivated by this level of accountability are the exact people who come to work at Acceleration Partners and stay. But accountability isn't just specific to our culture; it's a universal principle that benefits any organization. The whole organization performs better when every employee knows what is expected of them.

I believe that outcomes matter most, and the performance you get is determined by the metrics you measure. In my career, I never prioritized face time with managers or working exhausting hours to show commitment. Most top organizations recognize that it's most important for employees to achieve the outcomes they've committed to accomplish. This encourages employees to work smarter, not harder or longer.

We intuitively understand this in sales. No one cares how many calls a salesperson makes, meetings they take, or hours they work if there are no sales made at the end of the day. Salespeople are rewarded for their outputs, not their inputs. You would take a salesperson who sold $50K a day working two hours over one who sold $10K working twelve hours every day of the week and twice on Sunday.

Organizations that manage people through requiring face time or pushing for hefty time and effort inputs often do this because they either haven't set the proper outcome expectations or because they aren't capable of holding people accountable, and therefore this is the only metric they have to measure. This is where consistency and clarity come into play.

Consistency

Finally, we have the key modifiers to vision, values, and goals. The first is consistency—repeatedly following procedures that are proven to work and committing to uphold the standards that are essential for excellence. We have several consistent processes that keep us on track.

Our regular company, leadership, and team meetings all follow the same cadence. On company calls, departments present in the same order each time, we highlight examples of people who were recognized for demonstrating core values, and we repeat key messages that are core to our business. We don't have all-company daily huddles because we work across many time zones, but our teams each have weekly meetings, and our entire company joins the same call every other week.

Twice a year, we hold in-person gatherings called hub meetings, where we gather together all our employees in each of our geographic regions to share experiences and give feedback to our leadership teams. This hub strategy, which will be explained in detail in a later chapter, allows us to meet with the majority of the company in person over a two-week period, twice each year. We also hold an annual in-person meeting called AP Summit, where the entire company congregates near the end of the year—more on that later as well.

We have documented core processes for everything we do

on a recurring basis. We consistently tell our employees: if you don't know how to do something or you haven't done it before, we have a best practice that you should follow. That doesn't mean our core processes are completely rigid—as per our core value of **Excel and Improve**, we encourage anyone to find a way to improve these processes if they can—but we push people to share those changes with everyone as an upgrade to our operating system. That way, we ensure individual improvements are used by everybody else and elevate our best thinking.

If you want to build consistent processes and standards into your organization, I highly recommend using an alignment system, which is a system of tools and best practices. Two of the more well-known systems used by growth companies are Gazelles, which is detailed in Verne Harnish's excellent business growth book, *Scaling Up: How a Few Companies Make It…and Why the Rest Don't*, and EOS Worldwide, which is drawn from Gino Wickman's bestselling book, *Traction: Get a Grip on Your Business*. OKR, or objectives and key results, is also a popular system employed in many larger organizations.

These operating systems bring together hundreds of years of best practices around strategic planning, goal setting, execution, meeting cadence, and structure into a unified package. When implemented properly, these systems are the glue that helps hold your business together. They ensure everybody is operating according to proven standards and processes and is in alignment.

Clarity

The second key modifier is clarity, which starts with clarifying for employees what our vision, values, and goals are. Our employees can't do the work we need them to unless they really understand those core concepts and how they fit into the big picture.

Clarity starts even before they join our company. It's too common for job descriptions to be vague, filled with broad responsibilities, buzzwords, and even competing interests, such as "sales and marketing." In contrast, we want people to know in the application process what exactly will be expected of them if they're hired. Each of our position descriptions includes five core job responsibilities, which are the most essential duties employees must perform in that role. We also clarify the metrics and qualitative outcomes by which we would define success six and twelve months after hiring. There shouldn't be surprises in the performance reviews at these time periods—employees can look at their job description and know if they're measuring up to expectations.

When our managers review employees, they can evaluate

people objectively. It can be difficult for people to honestly evaluate employees they care for personally, so we've created a system where managers must specifically evaluate them against core values, quarterly goals, and core job responsibilities to determine whether the individuals are hitting the mark.

Clarity also extends to our organizational transparency. We have adopted open book management, not just on goals and metrics but on finances as well. If you want employees to advance the interests of the company, they need to understand the financial indicators that are crucial to the overall health of the business. We train each of our new hires on the financial metrics of the business, explaining what profit, cash flow, EBIT (Earnings Before Interest & Taxes), and other key indicators are, and we update the entire company on those financial numbers in our regular company calls. By being an open book, everybody knows where the company stands at any given time.

This isn't easy to do—pulling back the curtain on things like revenue and profit is a scary step for many leaders—but it goes a long way in clarifying the health and priorities of the organization. How can we hold people accountable for outcomes if they don't understand the financial implications of those goals? More importantly, financial transparency allows us to bring problems and opportunities to the entire team to solve, as they have the data and financial literacy needed to make the best decisions.

Another important point: clarity isn't just about explaining things well; it requires going to great lengths to ensure everybody understands the game and the rules. People need to hear the same thing multiple times to fully process it.

I underestimated this phenomenon for a long time. I had previously assumed people fully understood something I only said one or two times. This is where the Rule of Seven comes in. Legendary leadership thinker Patrick Lencioni insists that any CEO is also a CRO, or a chief repeating officer. Organizational leaders have to repeat things like vision, values, goals, and metrics several times to guarantee they are being absorbed by the full team. Seven times seems like a lot, but when you are steadily growing and constantly adding new people, that level of repetition is necessary to ensure sufficient comprehension.

All this adds up to a full picture of an organization—what we value, how we're performing, and where we see the company going in the future. Because we're upfront about these key characteristics, employees can decide if this is the organization they want to work for in the long term. And just as importantly, it goes a long way in helping to find, recruit, and hire the right talent to execute these core components to perfection.

4

What Starts Well

Once you know the culture you want to develop within your firm, recruiting becomes the single most important factor in evolving a healthy, high-performing culture. Most of the mistakes that you will make building your culture—and your business in general—will stem from hiring the wrong people. These mistakes are painful and expensive.

These are people who don't share your values and/or don't want to be held accountable for outcomes. If you hire the wrong person, especially for a remote environment, it's very hard to train them into being the right one. Training employees is vital, but training resources should be invested in helping high-potential hires grow and improve rather than helping poor culture or aptitude fits get to an average level. Some qualities, values, and characteristics that you are looking for may not be things that are easily changed in adults. You need to understand what can be trained and what needs to come as part of the package; it's often a matter of talent or characteristics versus skill. Good judgment is a characteristic. Microsoft Excel is a skill.

Like many facets of remote work, the key is to ensure you have the best possible hiring methods, interviewing techniques, and decision-making tactics for your hiring managers. Before we delve into the specific nuances of hiring remote workers and interviewing them virtually, we need to start by outlining a hiring strategy that works in all types of workplaces.

Create a Hiring System

For hiring, the biggest mistake organizational leaders can make is relying on instinct to determine whether a candidate is the right fit for their company. Part of effective leadership is understanding your limitations and knowing how to limit human error. As the popular saying goes, "In God we trust. All others must bring data."

While we'll explore how to hire people who will excel specifically in a remote work environment, the fact is that the best way to hire for a virtual organization is to do so effectively overall, something a majority of companies don't do very well today.

Companies that have rigorous, careful hiring methods can hire effectively in and for any environment.

No one has influenced my view on hiring more than Dr. Geoff Smart, CEO of ghSMART and coauthor of *Who: The A Method for Hiring*, the best book on talent acquisition in the marketplace.

Smart earned a PhD in the 1990s, studying under legendary management guru Peter Drucker at the Drucker School of Management at Claremont Graduate University. In Drucker's class, Smart created a business plan for a world-class consulting firm entirely focused on hiring and developing talent, and he fulfilled that vision with ghSMART.

After spending over twenty years analyzing talent acquisition data, creating analytical hiring strategies, and helping companies refine their hiring methods, Smart has come to a clear conclusion: most hiring managers really don't know what they're doing. In fact, many of them have been using their same ineffective approach for decades.

"There's a lot of homegrown interview questions or methods, and there's a very short list of approaches that work well," Smart said. "And it's not people's fault. We don't get trained on how to hire people in high school or college or even in most grad schools."

According to ghSMART's research, hiring managers

worldwide have only a 50 percent success rate. This sad reality means that the world's interviewers could flip a coin on any given hiring decision and get essentially the same outcome.

The reality is that even for the most perceptive leaders, there isn't a magic bullet hiring technique that indicates with certainty if someone has the specific temperament to thrive in a given culture, the essential skills to do the job at hand, and the aptitude to grow along with the organization over time. There definitely isn't one perfect interview question that will tell you everything you need to know about a candidate, especially today, when interview preparation resources help candidates master traditional questions and tell hiring interviewers what they want to hear.

"People always ask me, 'what are the magic interview questions?' or 'what's a great interview question?'" Smart said. "And it's not about the question. It's about the whole system. Otherwise, you don't get a good result."

If you learn nothing else from Smart and his team, know this: hiring is more science than art. Rather than relying on your own instincts, it's essential to create a hiring system that every hiring manager in your company can follow to minimize human error and make it easier for interviewers to do their due diligence. Otherwise, you might miss something vital that causes you to overlook the right candidate—or choose the wrong one.

Smart advises interviewers to not spend too much time asking candidates questions that are hypothetical or abstract in nature, the reason being that hypothetical questions usually result in hypothetical answers. Unfortunately, these types of questions tend to dominate job interviews. You've certainly been asked what your greatest strength is in a job interview, and you may have also been asked about what you might do in a future situation if you are hired. The answers to these questions really don't demonstrate how you will perform in the role or if you are a fit for the company's culture.

Instead, Smart says it's more effective to go through a candidate's employment history to get specific information about what they accomplished, what they've learned, how they worked with their managers, and even why they left. Often, these behavior-based questions—which are rooted in a candidate's concrete past experiences—can reveal qualities or tendencies that are highly predictive of future behavior and might completely change your view of the applicant. Not only do you have to ask the questions, you need to give the candidate time to answer fully and to keep probing for a deeper level of detail.

Smart also advises interviewers to frame these types of employment history questions by getting candidates to walk through their entire experience and paying close attention for details that warrant a follow-up question. Smart finds that if you ask employees to describe an instance where they demonstrated a particular quality, that gives them the opportunity to selectively share details from their past that paint them in the best possible light. A better way to get a fuller sense of a person's professional performance is to uncover the aspects of their professional life that they aren't as quick to share.

Smart's favorite example of exploring a candidate's past comes from an interview he conducted himself. Smart was digging through the candidate's professional history and asked why they'd left their most recent job. The gentleman replied that he'd had a difference of opinion with his CEO over the strategic direction of the company. Rather than accepting this interview-ready answer, Smart pressed for more details, using his technique of asking open-ended prompts such as "and then what happened?" and "tell me more," then waiting silently for the candidate to answer.

After responding to a few of those prompts, the candidate revealed that he'd insulted the company's CEO during a board meeting. A less-experienced interviewer might have stopped there, but Smart kept asking for more details. That's how he learned that the CEO fired the candidate in his office after the meeting. Most of us would have taken that answer and moved on, but an additional ask of "what happened next?" revealed that the candidate then slapped the CEO across the face and was therefore terminated for cause, resulting in the forfeiture of $3 million in stock options. The incident became known as the $3 million slap.

The candidate certainly had a difference of opinion with his CEO, and a violent one at that.

Imagine hiring an employee for your management team because you liked their answer to hypothetical questions, then only discovering later that they insulted their boss in front of his board and committed battery.

Smart wouldn't have learned that very important fact and story by asking the candidate what animal he most strongly identified with or where he saw himself in five years or even if he had taken an initial answer at face value and just moved on to the next question.

This approach extends to questioning employees about their prior remote work experience if they have it. If a candidate says they've enjoyed remote work in the past, don't just take that answer at face value; ask them what they liked about working from home, how they managed to stay productive, and what they did with the flexibility it afforded them.

Hiring disasters happen all too frequently, and these mistakes are perhaps more damaging in remote organizations where there is more autonomy and less supervision. If you hire someone without the skills to do the job on day one, it's hard to train them up to the level you need them to be at without the benefit of frequent in-person monitoring and coaching. One rule we have always followed at our company is that we never train with the goal to get someone to average.

It can be harder to realize that a new employee is a poor culture fit without seeing that person in action in the office those first few days and months. You won't see the eye rolls, hear them raise their voice inappropriately, or see them treating someone disrespectfully in the break room. You may not realize they're ineffective at motivating their team or unable to hold them accountable until after a few consecutive quarters of subpar performance. Most damagingly, you may only discover you can't trust them after they've alienated other employees, damaged client relationships, or made costly financial mistakes.

The best way to avoid this pitfall is to limit bias and human error with the type of hiring system that Smart teaches. You can incorporate Smart's blueprint and customize the system to account for the nuances of hiring remote workers and to reflect the core values you need your employees to emulate. Let's dig into the details of how to do this.

When we rely on intuition or gut feeling, we are more prone to hire people similar to ourselves or who share our strengths and weakness. This is not how you build a high-performing team. Instead, the best teams are people who share similar values but have complementary skills and characteristics.

We also often get attached to a candidate we like as a person but who won't excel in the role. I have actually found that it's better to trust your gut instincts *not* to hire someone, especially if there is something setting off your intuition that you can't quite put your finger on. However, it is never a good idea to rely solely on your instincts to hire someone unless you can back it up with evidence.

Often, hiring managers tend to be less scientifically rigorous the higher they are on the org chart. Organizational leaders, CEOs especially, frequently have their favorite unconventional interview questions, such as "What animal best represents you?" or "What do you see yourself doing in five years?" The problem is that these questions have no statistical validity; you might know you hired a few great people who answered "lion," but you have no idea if you missed potential great employees who had a different answer, because there is no control group.

Similarly, a candidate might have a great answer for their five-year vision that they have been giving for ten years and have made no progress toward. Hiring by instinct can work occasionally—every manager or leader can probably tell you about an unconventional hire they made who became a star—but when you play the averages, it leads to costly mistakes. Like gambling, you tend to hear about the winners much more than the losers.

To hire the right people, it's vital to first clarify what skills and attributes are needed for the role, what success looks like for the candidate, and the outcomes for which they will be responsible. Comprehensive job descriptions are crucial on this front; if an employee accepts a job without having an idea of what is expected of them, their early months—or years—at the organization will be marked by trial and error.

In contrast, a role description that clearly defines the job's responsibilities acts as a report card for every hire as part of a future performance review. When it comes time to evaluate a new hire's progress, there shouldn't be any surprises. When you're completely clear about what you're looking for from a new employee, you can determine early on if they're the right person rather than wasting years waiting to see if somebody will improve.

As I mentioned above, we try to remove human error and bias from the situation as much as possible by standardizing the process. Things like requiring values-based questions and aptitude testing for every single hire help build some objective criteria into hiring. To further standardize our process, we use a cloud-based applicant tracking system called Greenhouse, but there are many similar options in the market you should explore.

Our applicant tracking system is set up to allow interviewers to rate candidates numerically for each interview question, creating scorecards that other members of a hiring team can review.

Hiring can be filled with unconscious biases, and this type of system helps people compare their evaluation against those of others and make an informed, objective decision. The interviewer will have a specific guideline to rate answers on a scale from one to ten based on the quality of the response, with an example of what they should be listening for the candidate to say or not say.

Even if you aren't in the position to invest in this type of system, it's still helpful to have some kind of standard process for evaluating and comparing candidates. For example, even creating a spreadsheet that lists all the criteria in the job description and allows interviewers to give a numerical score for each one will add a degree of standardization to the process.

When the team comes together to make the final decision, they compare all scoring from the interview process against their original job description and hiring criteria. The other key practice in this final round, which comes out of a common practice in Silicon Valley, is to bring an unbiased third party who does not have the urgency of hiring for their own team into the process. They are there to wear the company hat and provide a check and balance. Because these people aren't as close to the hiring decision, they are often able to point out blind spots and areas where the team is overlooking the data about the candidate.

Finally, at the end of each hiring decision, the recruiter in charge will ask the hiring team if the candidate is better than 90 percent of the applications we have seen, if they will raise the bar for our team as a whole, and if someone is willing to be accountable for the hire. Hiring teams must affirm all three of these requirements before we make an offer.

Some candidates are hired at companies because no one strenuously objects anywhere in the process. We have tried to build a system where no one is hired unless someone strenuously advocates for them with accountability.

Conducting Virtual Interviews

During the pandemic, many organizations have been forced to quickly learn how to hire employees through video interviews. If you've never conducted a job interview without the candidate in the room, it may feel challenging to get a full sense of the person and visualize them as a prospective employee.

However, Smart argues that virtual interviewing doesn't have to be a roadblock to hiring effectively. In fact, he says that avoiding protracted in-person interviews—including ones that happen outside the office, such as at a restaurant or on a golf course—can actually push hiring managers more toward the unreliable realm of instinct and gut feeling. Organizations that are hiring through video should instead use that as a testing ground for the hiring system explained above.

"You need to have a really good interview method," Smart said. "It has to be fact-based, it has to be past-oriented, and you have to collect data."

When interviewing virtually, it's important to remember that you are seeing less of a person's body language. In an in-person interview, it's typically easier to determine if a question has caught a candidate off-balance or if they are avoiding telling the full story about a previous professional experience. Because of this, it's essential for video interviewers to pay close attention to what the person is saying to get a sense of when to ask a follow-up question or request more details.

While interviewing over a video call has some drawbacks, it also offers particular advantages for hiring employees for a remote organization. In some ways, this virtual method gives you a better sense of how the interviewee will perform in a virtual work environment. If a candidate is uncomfortable or ineffective when communicating over a video call, that may not bode well for their chances of excelling in a role where much of their communication may be increasingly virtual.

Virtual interviews also give you a chance to get a sense of the candidate's attention to detail in setting up their virtual workspace. We discussed in chapter 1 the necessity of setting up a professional workspace when working from home, and seeing how someone presents themselves in a video interview can be a good way to gauge how much thought and care they'll put into presenting themselves professionally once they actually join your team. If an interviewee is speaking to you from a noisy space, has an ineffective headset or microphone, or joins the call with a messy background, that tells you something about how they might present themselves in the future as a member of your team.

Hiring for a Remote Environment

Many skeptics express disbelief that remote companies such as ours have team members who are so productive and accountable while working from home. In these cases, they may be incorrectly assuming that all their people could make the same adjustment.

In reality, hiring employees for a remote culture requires a specialized approach, including identifying and hiring employees with specific characteristics that make them particularly adaptable to working from home. Specifically, the most effective remote companies evaluate candidates to determine if they can maintain their professional performance and their personal well-being while working virtually.

A candidate with prior experience of working from home can be a good predictor of future success. In some cases, we encounter applicants who have worked from home before—either full-time or a day or two each week—and know they enjoy it. However, you'll likely hire many people who have never worked outside a traditional office before, and therefore you will have to identify the characteristics and qualities outlined above that may not be obviously displayed in a candidate's previous experience.

If you're looking for questions to ask potential remote employees, here are some examples, for both candidates with prior remote experience and without.

BEHAVIORAL INTERVIEW QUESTIONS TO ASK CANDIDATES WITH REMOTE WORK EXPERIENCE

- ▸ What did the flexibility of remote work allow you to change about your life?
- ▸ Can you share a time when you struggled with a project because you weren't collaborating with your team in person and how you responded?
- ▸ When you first started working remotely, what were some of the things you missed about working in an office?
- ▸ Can you share an example of how you communicated effectively with colleagues without the opportunity to speak to them in person?
- ▸ What did you do to avoid feeling cooped up or isolated while working from home?

▸ What have you disliked most about working from home in the past?

BEHAVIORAL INTERVIEW QUESTIONS TO ASK CANDIDATES WITHOUT REMOTE WORK EXPERIENCE

▸ Was there ever a short period when you worked remotely, either from home or while traveling?

▸ What do you think is most valuable for you personally about working in an office, and what do you find most personally frustrating about it?

▸ Are there things you do outside work that are limited by your current work schedule?

▸ What changes in your lifestyle or work habits do you think working remotely would allow you to make?

It can also be very helpful to make a concerted effort to identify which attributes are necessary to thrive personally and professionally while working virtually in your organization. We've done this by talking to our employees who are working remotely for the first time and like it more than they expected, carefully debriefing the situations where newly remote employees struggled and ultimately left the organization, and observing patterns in both cases.

It's particularly crucial to consider two questions when evaluating potential remote employees. First, do they have the characteristics needed to work effectively in a virtual workplace? Second, will they be happy and fulfilled working from home over the long term?

The first question is related to innate personal and professional characteristics, while the second is related more to environmental preferences. Both factors determine whether a candidate will be able to fulfill their responsibilities and work well with others virtually. These are some of the essential professional characteristics to look for in remote candidates.

ESSENTIAL PROFESSIONAL CHARACTERISTICS FOR REMOTE EMPLOYEES

- **Self-motivated:** ability to work effectively and consistently without in-person oversight.
- **Self-directed:** ability to figure out problems proactively and avoid getting stuck.
- **Strong communicator:** communicating in a virtual workplace requires more care and clarity than in an office environment. Value people who can communicate clearly to others across different modalities and who listen well to others.
- **Self-confident:** ability to work consistently without frequent validation of their work and decision-making.

Because remote employees can't check in with management as frequently as in an office, they must be able to confidently execute their daily tasks without oversight.

▶ **Accountable:** tendency to achieve assigned outcomes, take ownership of tasks, and take responsibility when outcomes are not met.

Smart concurs with several attributes on this list. His team at ghSMART is completely remote, so he's overseen a considerable amount of hiring for his own virtual team in addition to helping the firm's clients do the same. Smart has found that remote employees are most likely to succeed when they are self-sufficient, capable of managing their time well, and able to stay on top of their workload without constant reminders or follow-ups.

"You're looking for proactivity and self-reliance," Smart said. "If they were in a remote setting before, ask them, how did you do? What were your targets? What did you accomplish, and how did you accomplish it? Tell me about the people you worked with. Ask all that normal stuff; just ask about it in a remote context. And listen to what they say."

Beyond these core competencies, it's also important to recognize that not everybody will be fulfilled working from home, and the adjustment can be impossible for some people.

You'll even encounter people who are highly effective working remotely but simply don't enjoy it and aren't able to stay in your organization for long.

One consistent theme we've seen among employees who adapt well to remote work is an affinity toward flexibility. These people have something in their life—whether they're a working parent, a competitive athlete, or an avid traveler—that makes them enjoy being removed from the rigid boundaries of an office and a nine-to-five schedule. For these people, the autonomy to structure a work-life integration that works for them is a personal priority, and they're willing to pass up a traditional office environment to get it. If you asked them why they wanted the job, flexibility would be in their top five reasons. For people who prefer an office, it usually doesn't make the top five.

COMMON ENVIRONMENTAL PREFERENCES OF CANDIDATES WHO WILL BE FULFILLED WORKING REMOTELY

- ▶ Interested in professional autonomy and the ability to set their own schedule and find a workflow that suits them
- ▶ Values flexibility, including the ability to travel and work from wherever they want
- ▶ A working parent who needs flexibility for pickup and drop-off, does not want a commute, and/or wants to design a

work routine that allows them to be more present with their family

▸ A competitive athlete/performer with a dedicated practice routine and/or competes in events

▸ Enjoys digging into a task without interruption or distraction

▸ Has a full social life outside work and doesn't need work as the basis for social connections

For people who would rather work in an office and who don't value that flexibility, the chances of success are much lower. One type of person who we've learned to identify during hiring is the social butterfly. This is the extreme extrovert who gets their energy from being around other people all day, who wants that in-person connection and really struggles being alone for extended periods.

This is not to say in the least that we have a company full of introverts—far from it. However, while most people can adapt well to remote work, social butterflies have a hard time in a remote work environment because they'll be missing a crucial part of their desired work and life experience: frequent social interaction. It's better for everybody involved not to assume any person can simply acclimatize happily to working from home.

If your company has clearly defined core values, you need to assess whether candidates truly possess those values, not whether they like them. Core values describe the DNA of someone who will be successful in a company's culture. For example, our values of **Own It**, **Excel and Improve**, and **Embrace Relationships** are the principles, policies, and procedures for our culture at Acceleration Partners, one that prioritizes accountability, teamwork, constant improvement, and flexibility.

Our values align closely with attributes that are needed in the remote workplace, particularly **Own It**. When you aren't connected in person, it's important to know your employees can work independently while still advancing the company toward its goals and upholding its values in everything they do. Over time, we've figured out which traits tend to indicate a prospective employee will do well in our remote environment.

Geoff Smart supports this need to build your hiring around your culture's principles, saying, "Put what's special about your culture on the scorecard, the buzzwords of your own firm. 'Whereas other firms are X, we want to be Y.' We're going to put that on the scorecard to make sure we hire people who match the culture, because at least half the reason mis-hires happen is due to culture, not due to a technical deficit."

The reality is that for our account manager roles, which are about 90 percent of our hiring, we hire only 1–2 percent of the applicants who apply for each position. Our culture and working style aren't for everyone, but what we have done is build a system to specifically identify the 1–2 percent of people who will thrive in it. It's taken almost ten years to do that well.

This is why you have to take time to honestly evaluate your organizational culture and make adjustments where necessary. When your company's values and objectives are clearly defined, it's easier to identify what types of employees can thrive in that environment, even with limited supervision. The biggest difference between managing a virtual team and an in-person one is that you can't afford to leave these things to chance. By determining exactly what you need from your team, you'll make smarter hiring decisions and build a stronger organization—even in a remote workplace.

5

Setting Your Team Up for Success

Many successful companies with a distributed workforce share similar characteristics. They're often nimble and entrepreneurial and embrace remote work as an effective, efficient way to access a broader talent pool while reducing overhead costs.

Leadership teams within larger organizations that tend to have long-established in-office cultures are perhaps the most skeptical of remote work. They assume the model could never work for businesses of their scale, processes, or workforce size.

Once a member of this school of thought, Vel Dhinagaravel completely changed his viewpoint when COVID-19 forced him to make his entire company remote.

Dhinagaravel is the founder and CEO of Beroe Inc., a procurement intelligence firm with five hundred employees in the

United States and India. Between 2015 and early 2020, only twenty-five employees worked virtually. When the pandemic hit in March 2020, Beroe made the decision to send the entire five-hundred-person team home to work remotely.

Like many company leaders at that time, Dhinagaravel was initially concerned that remote work couldn't work for Beroe. He was concerned that communications would break down without an office holding the team together and that productivity would dip.

Despite the abrupt transition to a fully virtual workplace, what's surprised Dhinagaravel is the increases in Beroe's productivity, employee retention, and engagement since the shift. Employees are getting more done, communicating effectively, and, in most cases, improving their work-life integration.

One key reason for this is that the company has been aggressively rethinking and updating its operational playbook to adapt to a virtual environment.

Dhinagaravel and his team trained managers to proactively communicate and check in with their employees, including holding daily video conferences with their teams and biweekly one-on-one calls with their direct reports. Their HR team began calling every single employee once every two weeks to ensure they felt supported and connected. Beroe also invested in multiple digital tools for employees to easily communicate with one another and with leadership.

Having seen firsthand how effective remote work could be for his entire organization, Dhinagaravel now anticipates 30 to 40 percent of Beroe employees will continue working from home permanently. His company has demonstrated that leaders' concerns about taking their companies virtual can often be addressed and mitigated with thoughtful, proactive changes to their communication procedures, management tactics, and technological infrastructure.

The biggest mistake an organization can make with remote employees is leaving their workers to figure these things out for themselves, especially if they have never worked remotely before. Giving employees a list of best practices—such as the ones detailed in chapter 2—is helpful, but those things alone won't necessarily lead to top-tier remote performance.

In this chapter, we'll explore the specific systems, methodologies, tools, and techniques that make remote work more seamless for employees and more productive for organizations of all sizes.

Comprehensive Onboarding

When I started my first job at twenty-two, I had an experience that will be familiar to many employees. Neither HR nor my boss realized I was starting that day, so when I arrived, they didn't have a computer ready for me, and the only direction I received was, "Just shadow Winnifer."

Winnifer actually became a good friend of mine, but that friendship was the only positive outcome from the onboarding experience. The reality is that a lot of companies get away with this sort of onboarding only because they are in an office and can tell new employees simply to tag along with someone else. While this approach shouldn't be acceptable for any organization, this unstructured approach to onboarding new employees would be disastrous for remote organizations.

New employees need—and deserve—to start off strong when they begin at a company. They should be given the tools, training, and technology they need to excel and to know who to turn to when they need help.

Onboarding is where remote companies are at an inherent disadvantage and must be more intentional with their approach. We have taken that disadvantage and turned it into a strength. We've created an onboarding program that I believe would be the envy of many larger organizations, remote or otherwise.

To give you a sense of this, when a new hire starts at Acceleration Partners, they are provided with a comprehensive onboarding calendar. Essentially, this is an agenda that lays out what meetings they'll need to attend in the first few weeks on the job, who they'll shadow and learn from as a part of their training path, when the mandatory all-company meetings are, and other detailed plans. In addition to this onboarding schedule, team members throughout the organization in various countries reach out to offer their help and to welcome them.

DAY ONE

9AM–10AM	Onboarding with HR
10AM–11AM	Call with manager
11AM–12PM	Training process overview
12PM–1PM	Lunch
1PM–5PM	Learning management system (LMS) course review time (complete preassigned courses)

DAY TWO

9AM–10AM	Call with manager
10AM–11AM	Meet the team
11AM–12PM	Review employee handbook
12PM–1PM	Lunch
1PM–2PM	All-company call
2PM–5PM	LMS course review time (complete preassigned courses)

DAY THREE

9AM–10AM	Call with manager

10AM–11AM	Set up digital tools
11AM–12PM	Job training call
12PM–1PM	Lunch
1PM–2PM	Company finance overview
2PM–3PM	Company culture overview
3PM–5PM	LMS course review time (complete preassigned courses)

DAY FOUR

9AM–10AM	Call with manager
10AM–11AM	Job training call A
11AM–12PM	Job training call B
12PM–1PM	Lunch
1PM–2PM	Company compliance overview
2PM–3PM	Weekly team meeting
3PM–4PM	Company technology overview
4PM–5PM	LMS course review time (complete preassigned courses)

Organizations with remote employees can't leave onboarding to chance. In an office, an employee may be able to learn by asking people for help and observing others. However, in a remote environment, an employee will likely end up just sitting alone at their computer with no idea what to do or where to start. No matter how much of a "go-getter" a person is, this is not an effective or empowering way to get them started.

Top remote organizations, on the other hand, prioritize onboarding and build meticulously detailed training programs because they are key to employees' short- and long-term success within the organization. If you don't get your training right, you're setting up new virtual employees for failure.

Meetings and Availability

You can learn a lot from the pioneers of an industry or strategy. In remote work, that is Jason Fried, cofounder and CEO of the popular project management tool Basecamp. Basecamp sells a collaboration software tool that features shared to-do lists, detailed project plan templates, file storage, shared document editing, and a chat function. The company has fifty-seven employees but serves millions of users at over 120,000 organizations worldwide.

Fried has led a remote team for over twenty years, and the company has been profitable for its entire existence, even while working in the occasionally tumultuous tech world. Fried and his business partner, David Heinemeier Hansson, have also written several books about workplace innovation, including *Remote: Office Not Required.*

While most tech companies are known for long hours, sprawling open-plan offices, and the constant chatter of in-person collaboration, Basecamp takes a decidedly different approach, including becoming one of the first software companies to openly adopt the remote model. Today, they have a global team of employees who work from wherever they want, are required to work no more than forty hours per week, and only need to work for four days during the summer.

Fried and his team work half as much as some of their competitors but get more done; their approach to remote work is a big reason why. According to Fried, remote work allows easier access to a state he likes to call "REM work." And while it is, by Fried's own admission, an unscientific term, the analogy makes sense.

"A good night's sleep is when you go to sleep at, let's say nine, and wake up at seven or eight and say, 'wow, I slept through the night, that's awesome,'" Fried said. "That's what a good workday should look like. You should be able to say, 'I had a good workday. I wasn't interrupted. I wasn't distracted all day. I had an eight-hour day to myself to focus on work.'"

Essentially, it's easier to be productive when you can focus on your projects and tasks for extended periods of time without interruption. An eight-hour workday where you have two-to three-hour blocks of uninterrupted work time and all your breaks are planned into your schedule is bound to be more productive than a workday where people constantly break your concentration whenever you get into a focused groove.

The esteemed economist Vilfredo Pareto found that 80 percent of our outcomes come from 20 percent of our actions. For example, 80 percent of our sales come from 20 percent of our clients. This Pareto principle—often referred to as the 80/20 rule—suggests that you'll get a significant portion of your work accomplished in those short stretches when you are in an uninterrupted state of flow. We must be aware of the importance of these periods of uninterrupted work and understand what we lose when we are interrupted.

"If you're at work, and your head's down on a task and someone pulls you aside for something, that just cut your moment in half," Fried said. "When you get back to work, you're not right back into that thought. You have to slowly get back into that mindset again."

Anyone who's worked in an office knows just how difficult it can be to give your uninterrupted attention to a task. Evidence shows that human attention spans have become shorter than that of a goldfish, and working in an office can exacerbate the problem.[1]

Whether it's a colleague stopping by your office to ask a question, an undercurrent of noise, or even the glimpse of a person walking through your peripheral vision, today's offices are rife with things to keep you from focusing deeply on work.

Part of why remote work is perfect for Basecamp is that Fried wants his team to have long stretches of uninterrupted time to focus on work. This includes a somewhat rare strategy of not allowing employees to share calendars to facilitate meetings. Contrary to conventional wisdom, Fried wants to make it harder to create meetings, not easier.

"Most businesses have shared calendars where you can see everyone else's schedule. And if you want to get on someone else's calendar, you just click a box and it fills in with color and sends an invite," Fried said. "And it makes it so easy to take other people's time. And that's the problem."

Even scheduled meetings can be detrimental to productivity. If you spend six hours in meetings, that only leaves two hours in a standard workday for focused project time. You've probably felt the mild anxiety that sets in when you start working and realize most of your day is blocked off for meetings. It's easy to be struck by a fear that you won't be able to get your actual work done.

It feels rude to decline a meeting request, even if you have a lot to do. Most employees want to be team players who their colleagues can count on for collaboration or brainstorming. And remote employees may feel this pressure more acutely; they may be worried that if they're constantly avoiding meetings and protecting their time, their colleagues will either label them as aloof, question how they are spending their time, or, even worse, forget them entirely. As Fried indicates, it's easier for employees to block off time for focused work when their calendars aren't overloaded with meetings. As a leader, a huge part of setting an effective culture is developing a meeting strategy and cadence that strikes a balance between helping employees collaborate and connect and giving them quality uninterrupted time to work on projects and deliverables.

It's possible to be both accessible and productive by determining in your schedule when you'll be working without interruption and when you are available to respond to colleagues. Leaders should encourage employees to set aside blocks of time in their calendars for focused work and remind workers that it's important to give colleagues that uninterrupted time.

One of my mentors, Warren Rustand, who has been chairman or CEO of seventeen companies throughout an illustrious career, has a clear policy on how he manages his availability and use of time. He tells his team, "I have an open-door policy, but my door is not always open." Instead, he has regular check-ins and predetermined blocks of time on his calendar when he makes himself available. Rustand then encourages his team to consolidate issues that are not urgent into a list and to discuss these with him during those times.

An added benefit of this time delay is that Rustand finds his employees are able to resolve the majority of these issues before the meeting actually happens. It's an excellent combination of delegation and empowerment packaged as part of a time-management practice.

It's also important not to assume that the formats you may be familiar or comfortable with for an in-person meeting will naturally transfer to a virtual environment. While video conferences approximate in-person meetings, it's more difficult to keep attendees' attention and engagement in a virtual format. Fortunately, what many of us with a distributed workforce have come to discover is that many in-person meetings are far less necessary and even less effective in a remote workplace.

Transitioning to remote work is the perfect time to take stock of your meeting strategies. Meetings in an office often become a default—it's easier to have a colleague stop by your office for fifteen minutes to figure something out rather than passing emails back and forth for an hour.

Over time, many remote organizations find themselves holding fewer meetings than in-person organizations. Virtual meetings are harder to schedule, and it can be more difficult to know whether you're interrupting your colleagues' workflow. Remote teams often learn to collaborate without frequent meetings when given time to figure out what works for them.

However, organizations that suddenly found themselves working remotely during the pandemic went against this trend by holding more group calls and meetings than they had done in person in the office. In a study, Microsoft found that employees were conducting 55 percent more calls while working from home, which is correlated with an increase in stress levels.[2]

Without guidance, employees are likely to hold more meetings when working from home. This is why it's essential for the leaders of virtual teams to proactively determine and set expectations about which meetings are necessary and which are not.

As an analogy, consider how when you move from one home to another, you realize you own some personal items or even furniture that you don't need or want. Likewise, the transition to remote work can be an opportunity for organizations to evaluate which meetings you actually need and which just waste time and energy.

If you need to brainstorm ideas or have an important discussion on a core company focus, that calls for a meeting. But many people hold meetings to share information that could be conveyed via an email or an asynchronous video.

A great way to take stock of meeting efficacy is to consistently and honestly rate your meetings when they are done. There is a great practice you can borrow from the EOS, which calls key meetings "Level 10 Meetings." The premise is that at the end of every meeting, each attendee rates the meeting on a scale from one to ten. If the meeting isn't scoring a consistent average rating of nine or ten, it's not adding value, and you should improve it or scrap it.

Another useful tool is to assign a financial value to each meeting based on the length and number of employees invited and put that amount in the meeting invite. This creates awareness about the time value of meetings and tends to shorten the guest list.

In addition to cutting out some of your meetings, it's also highly advisable to adjust the format and length of meetings you still hold to maximize impact. It helps to keep virtual meetings shorter when possible, but it's also crucial to ensure that no single person is speaking uninterrupted for too long. Otherwise, it's not a meeting, it's a monologue, and employees will inevitably stop listening.

The meetings that waste the most time for organizations are what I call "update meetings." These meetings are especially ineffective in a remote environment. Update meetings are when a single or small number of speakers read a bunch of information, often from notes or sharing a PowerPoint deck, that could have been sent to attendees in advance or as a written memo. There is very little discussion or interactivity in these meetings, and they often feel like a waste of valuable time.

The only useful update meetings I have encountered are

those for the full company. These give employees an opportunity to hear what's happening outside their team or department and provide the full team with more access to leadership. Because these updates are valuable for the entire team to hear and it is difficult to have discussion-oriented meetings with all members of the company, update meetings can be effective in this context at the right intervals.

But for meetings involving teams or even departments, update meetings aren't the best way to share information. Even if the information is important, it's often presented in such a dry way that team members pay minimal attention, which defeats the purpose of the call in the first place. There are better ways to keep your team in the loop and hold people accountable.

One such way is the memo system, an approach most recently popularized by Amazon CEO Jeff Bezos. Bezos doesn't like meetings that focus on PowerPoint presentations or where people monologue through updates. At Amazon, Bezos requires team members to create a written memo before each meeting that provides the background material and information relevant for discussion. The memo is then distributed to all attendees at the beginning of the meeting, and everyone takes the time to read it, take notes, and prepare questions for discussion. Only after that does the meeting begin, with all attendees prepared to participate fully.

SAMPLE MEMO AGENDAS—THREE APPROACHES

Update/Status Memo

→ Summary of key data or performance indicators

→ Analysis of the key takeaways from the data

→ Areas of opportunity based on data

→ Red flags/areas of concern

→ Key discussion points for the meeting (what you actually need to discuss)

→ Outcomes required from the meeting

New Idea Memo

→ Overview of the current status or situation

→ The opportunity the idea pursues

→ The proposed plan to execute the idea

→ The resources needed to execute the idea

→ The risks associated with the idea

→ Next steps and action items for the idea

Debrief Memo

→ Describe the incident.

→ What went right/wrong?

→ What topic/department did the incident affect?

→ How was the issue addressed in the short term?

→ What was the outcome?

→ Are there any next steps from the incident?

> → What can we learn from the incident or apply to a new or existing core process?
>
> → Which other teams or departments need to be involved in changes?

We have modified this system for our remote environment at Acceleration Partners. Memos are sent out to the relevant team members before the meeting, and employees are expected to arrive having read the memo and prepared to discuss. The memo itself reduces the time needed for the meeting by at least half, and productivity and engagement are much higher as a result.

Meetings should be for interaction and conversation, and providing points for discussion in advance encourages employees to form their response, which is the point of a meeting in the first place.

Here's a good rule: if your meeting involves one person talking 90 percent of the time, it should have been replaced with an email memo or video message. Taking the time to schedule a meeting where participants don't actively engage with the content is a waste of valuable time and resources.

People don't have the energy to sit on video calls all day. By using the memo system to deliver information and make meetings shorter and more discussion-oriented, you can drive better engagement and productivity with your virtual meetings.

Similarly, it's useful to consider the proper cadence for meetings between managers and direct reports. In an office, managers may have direct reports join them for a fifteen-minute check-in over coffee each morning or have hour-long meetings once a week. When leading a virtual team, you may find it better to cut down or consolidate these meeting times to help clear your employees' schedules for project time and to avoid adding to video-call fatigue.

Executive Team Offsites

Some of the most important meetings that remote organizations can hold are executive team offsites. These annual, semiannual, or quarterly strategy and departmental meetings are a chance for a company's senior leaders and teams to congregate for bonding and strategic planning.

Even if you haven't been to one of these yourself, you can probably visualize it—a conference room covered with large Post-it notes, adrenaline-focused bonding activities like trust falls and bungee jumping, and an outside facilitator.

To maximize the impact of these meetings and to make time for team-building activities, it's very common for these offsites to last two or three days. They usually or often take place outside the standard work environment, ideally in a retreat-like setting.

As many companies learned during COVID-19, this is not an experience that is easily recreated online. Trying to use the same format and time parameters, including spending entire eight-hour days on video, will thoroughly exhaust your team. We made this mistake with our first virtual offsite in the early weeks of the pandemic, and the feedback from our leadership team was very poor.

While in-person executive offsites will likely be some of the first events to resume once people can travel freely, many organizations will need to figure out how to execute these valuable planning sessions virtually for the foreseeable future.

Here are a few best practices for creating the best possible virtual offsite:

- Start by cutting the total time of the meeting agenda in half. We covered video-call fatigue earlier, and your team's ideas and discussion will get less creative and insightful the longer they are stuck in a draining video conference. If the offsite must take place over multiple days, consider using only half of each day for the meeting.

- Start the night before the actual meeting with a meaningful icebreaker and one or two hours of high-level discussion that kick things off and ease the team into the meeting.

- End that first night with a virtual happy hour; perhaps play an interactive game or create a similarly social activity for the team. Of course, this will never replicate an in-person dinner, but it's the best way we have found to help the team build camaraderie when everyone is not in the same room. We also learned a lot about each other through the games, and on a few occasions, we laughed to the point of tears.

▸ Begin the more rigorous, detailed agenda the next morning. It's often best to start early in the morning, no later than 8:00 a.m., which is more feasible because everyone is already at home and hasn't spent the previous day traveling.

▸ Cut the day into blocks of two or three hours, with an hour-long break in between each one, rather than using a marathon meeting strategy that a team would use in person.

▸ Team members should use these pauses in the agenda to step away from their computers and take a clarity break rather than just rushing to answer emails. This could mean taking a walk outside, reading a book, or listening to music for an hour. Ideally, it should be something that helps you and the rest of the group return to the meeting refreshed and ready to engage in what are usually very important strategic discussions.

▸ Build in time to decompress. Arrange the agenda so your team doesn't work late into the afternoon. For example, the meeting can run from 8:00 a.m. to 11:00 a.m. with an hour-long break until noon, then resume for three more hours until 3:00 p.m. with short breaks throughout the meeting blocks. Then, the team gets the rest of the day off, allowing for a chance to decompress after several hours of strategic planning.

While this virtual experience doesn't replicate the experience of a multiday, in-person offsite, it's a good solution for situations where it's not possible to gather the full team or C-suite executives in one place. It's far better than skipping these important meetings altogether. In fact, your team may decide they like this style better and divide in-person strategy meetings into smaller chunks to avoid the common practice of a marathon session that wears everyone out.

Time Zone Etiquette

As companies increase their remote presence, they are more likely to have employees across different time zones. While it's easy to coordinate teams in time zones that are only an hour or two apart, it becomes much harder with employees scattered across the world.

At Acceleration Partners, while most of our team is in the United States, we have pockets of employees in Europe, Asia, and Australia as well. We have employees as far apart as America's

Pacific time zone and Australia's eastern time zone, a difference of eighteen hours. If your business is global, you may be in a similar situation, or you could be sooner than you think.

It's important to think globally and be mindful that others may work in drastically different time zones. We have realized this and have set the expectations that members of our Asia-Pacific team don't have to join our all-company meetings. Instead, we record them for them to watch back at a more convenient time.

We also have our Asia-Pacific team join regular live calls with our European team to add connectivity. For smaller team meetings or if you are joining a colleague or customer from another part of the world, take note of what time it is in their region. Resources like timeanddate.com make it easier than ever to determine what time it is around the world.

Many people who have not worked globally before tend to view the world through the lens of their own time zone. For example, if a predominantly UK-based team with one to two American employees insists on holding a meeting in the morning, they're effectively forcing the Americans to either miss the meeting or join before sunrise in their time zone. This type of decision may make the American employees feel undervalued or disconnected from their colleagues.

If it's morning or afternoon where you are and you're meeting with someone in a region where it is already evening, take a moment to thank them for joining after their workday, then offer to hold a future call at a more convenient time for them or occasionally rotate meeting times so the same employees aren't always joining at an inconvenient time. These types of small gestures go a long way toward making everyone feel valued and respected.

You might also consider using the delayed-delivery setting when sending emails to employees in different time zones. If you constantly send emails that arrive outside their normal working hours, it's likely to create an overwhelming feeling, and they may feel compelled to reply immediately. In contrast, if you delay the email delivery until the working hours of the recipient's time zone, they'll be less likely to feel that they're starting the day behind or that they can't shut down.

Finally, if you are confirming a meeting with someone in a different time zone, it's important to clarify which time zone you are referring to over email and ideally to confirm both simultaneously. So rather than asking if a colleague can meet at 3:00 p.m. and leaving it at that, write something along the lines of "are we on for 3:00 p.m. GMT/10:00 a.m. EST?" This will ensure the recipient knows what you mean, which then avoids an awkward situation where someone shows up at the wrong time. This happens all too frequently. It even happened when arranging a call with my editor as I wrote this book!

Travel Strategy

The COVID-19 pandemic has forced leaders and employees in all industries to challenge their business assumptions. Perhaps most surprisingly, sales teams have managed to close deals without meeting prospects in person, something that would've been unthinkable before the pandemic, especially in cultures and industries where face-to-face meetings are highly valued.

Anyone who has worked in sales at a company knows the standard formula: a salesperson identifies potential prospects, then travels to make an in-person pitch. Most traditional sales techniques are focused on commanding attention in the room and building relationships in person, allowing teams to close deals by creating a connection of trust.

Many organizations still consider in-person pitches to be very important and are eager to resume them after the pandemic passes. However, companies should consider whether it's necessary to hold an in-person meeting for every potential sale. While video calls can't entirely replicate an in-person pitch, they are far superior to a formal pitch done over a phone call. A video call at least allows salespeople to make a visual connection with the client and to present a sales deck via screen sharing.

It's also worth considering that current or potential clients may be more dispersed than before the pandemic. Part of the benefit of traveling to a client or prospect was to meet their team in person and build relationships beyond the main point of contact. But as remote work grows more prevalent, it's very possible that your prospect or client's team may not all be in an office or even have an office to visit.

While some companies will be eager to ramp up to their prepandemic travel practices, others will question whether it is worth the time and money. Salespeople may consider reserving travel for their most valuable prospects and reallocating the money from their travel budget into new and different tactics. Likewise, teams that support existing clients will also need to adapt their strategies and approach for how to build that same level of connection.

Team Building and Virtual Bonding

Team building has been a staple of organizations of all sizes for years. But in a fully remote world, companies have shifted from in-person activities like trust falls and obstacle courses to virtual activities that bring the company closer together in an unconventional way.

These organizations will likely be turning to companies like Kristi Herold's. Herold is the founder and CEO of the Sport & Social Club, a Canadian organization that historically coordinated recreational sports leagues for adults. Having built a brand based on bringing people together through play, Herold and her team made a quick pivot to facilitating virtual team-building activities for companies around the world when the pandemic hit. They launched a new offshoot of their business called JAM (workplayjam.com), which is entirely focused on remote activities.

JAM offers virtual games like bingo, trivia, digital scavenger hunts, and online escape rooms. They provide their own game hosts and arrange all the technology, so teams just have to show up and have fun. To add some customization for clients, Herold's team can even design their games to specifically reference the client company—trivia questions that relate to the company's history, bingo tiles that are named for departments and teams, and more. Herold's team even offers companies onboarding-focused games for new employees. New hires can quiz their new colleagues on trivia about themselves, learn about their new organization, and shorten their learning curve in a fun, entertaining way.

In the past, companies have consolidated all their team building into big, in-person activities, such as annual company retreats or parties. But the worldwide remote work experiment has brought with it a new trend of virtual team building, where companies can help their employees get to know one another and build camaraderie without having to spend the time and resources bringing everyone together. Rather than investing in an enormous in-person team-building exercise once a year, remote organizations may decide they're better off holding more frequent virtual gatherings instead.

Many newly remote organizations aren't sure how to facilitate personal connections between their suddenly virtual employees. Herold has faced this challenge with her own team, which is also now working virtually for the first time. It's difficult to replicate the organic, spontaneous banter of a workplace lunch or an office happy hour in a virtual setting.

However, these connections can often be facilitated with more thoroughly planned social activities. Virtual team-building events like the ones Herold and her team lead aren't dependent on employees attempting to have normal bonding conversations in a remote activity. Instead, they participate in an interactive game where everyone is given a chance to engage, and the activity is structured to avoid the awkwardness that can occasionally come with virtual bonding.

While we don't know how teams will handle their team-building activities in the future, it's possible that this is another area where leaders will see many of their previous assumptions challenged and adopt new practices. Maybe it's not always necessary to bring everyone together in one place to hold an impactful team-building exercise. There's plenty of opportunity for virtual team-building companies to grab a bigger share of what is likely to be a fast-growing market.

Technology

Employees make significant adjustments when working from home for the first time. For most organizations, it will be necessary to commit to making remote work as effective and functional as possible. That involves making significant investments in technology, including leveraging the many software tools on offer to help improve employee communications and user experience. Most of these resources are available in the cloud now, so materials can be instantly downloaded and installed.

I'll share several tech tools that many organizations have depended on while transitioning to remote work, all of which are cloud-based and require no hardware or major upfront capital investment. While these are great examples, there are many other tools available for each of these functions, so you can find what works best for you and your team.

SINGLE SIGN-ON

First, it's helpful to use a single sign-on (SSO) program, which is similar to a commercial version of a password manager. With all the technology platforms available today, it can become a huge hassle for employees to have to manage dozens of individual application accounts. With an SSO, employees can access a full suite of applications with a single login.

The more logins your team needs to remember and use, the less likely they are to use these tools. An SSO platform connects a large number of cloud-based applications to a single login, which makes things far more convenient. Our team currently uses Idaptive for this, but there are plenty of other strong players, including Okta and OneLogin.

When looking at these types of SSO tools, it can be helpful to pick one that requires two-factor authentication, such as requiring an employee to receive a code via text or email to sign in. This is a useful way to provide an extra layer of security and to protect company data in case someone's password is compromised or their electronic device is stolen.

CLOUD-BASED FILE SHARING

File sharing is crucial. An organization needs a secure platform that safely stores files with the appropriate file and folder permissions. It should also allow people to easily review and collaborate on documents and create a local folder on their computer for easy file access. Constantly passing documents back and forth via email and having employees save everything on their personal computer hard drives is a data management and security nightmare, and it also creates extra administrative work for employees.

Organizations with several teams and departments should use a platform that offers more granular file permissions so some folders and subfolders can be kept secure whereas others can be made public to entire teams, departments, or individuals. SharePoint, Box, and Egnyte are excellent examples for larger firms that need sophisticated folder protections.

Even small organizations need some type of cloud-based file sharing though. If you're a business of one, it's still essential to have a secure place to store files in the event of catastrophic computer failure. It's backbreaking for any size business to lose vital client information, process documents, or accounting books because someone spilled coffee on a laptop. If anything, the risk is more acute for smaller companies—the fewer employees you have, the more likely it is that any given worker is going to have irreplaceable or confidential files on their computer. Smaller companies or solo entrepreneurs can use simpler programs like Dropbox and Google Workspace.

LEARNING AND KNOWLEDGE MANAGEMENT

As discussed earlier, training and onboarding are critical components for remote organizations. It's important to have learning resources centralized in one place where employees can review them on demand rather than constantly scheduling training and learning calls.

This is where a learning management system (LMS) comes into play. An LMS is a platform where organizations can upload video and written training content for the entire company to review in their own time.

Many LMS programs allow you to add assessments to ensure everyone who needs to take a course does so and can go back if necessary to review the information. This is especially helpful for making sure employees take—and pass—essential assessments that everyone within the organization needs to know, such as a data security policy for the company.

An LMS allows managers to point employees to preexisting resources to get the training they need without having to set up a training call. A robust LMS also ensures that the company doesn't lose vital knowledge or training resources when key employees leave the organization. There's nothing worse than having an employee leave a company only to discover that nobody else on their team knows how to fulfill the departing person's duties or manage a process for which they were solely responsible.

A similarly useful tool is a knowledge management system (KMS), which is sometimes referred to as knowledge base software (KBS). A KMS or KBS allows teams to upload resources for the entire company that will answer frequently asked questions, provide generally applicable knowledge, and outline company policies and best practices. Our team uses the KBS Guru. One of Guru's best features is a validation system to ensure information is kept up-to-date. After a certain amount of time, Guru cards are marked red instead of green to notify users that the information may not be accurate. Experts in the various subject matters can then review these cards and verify that the information is accurate, ensuring that all information is trustworthy and updated.

A KBS offers similar benefits to employees. If an organization invests in a KBS and commits to keeping it updated, employees can easily access information on everything from HR benefits to filling out expense reports to core job processes. Think of it as your internal frequently asked questions document.

In a remote workplace, where employees don't regularly see finance or HR experts around the office or can't stop by someone's office to ask a quick question, a real-time database of this type of information is even more important. These centralized training and knowledge management resources are crucial to employees' success, especially if they're new to an organization.

HR SYSTEMS

In the previous chapter, I discussed the use of applicant tracking systems to streamline the management of recruiting and hiring, but it's also important to have centralized HR resources, including for essential functions such as managing employee time-off requests, hiring new staff, and carrying out performance evaluations. Centralizing these functions with tech tools makes it easier for managers to keep everything organized without having to spend time tracking people's time off and other HR needs.

These resources include the following:

▸ An online tool for managing your HR administration functions (start date, salary history, time-off management, personal info, etc.). For most small- and medium-sized businesses, this was done for years in a massive HR Excel spreadsheet. Today, especially in a remote work environment, a more sophisticated structure is required. We use BambooHR to house and manage many of these elements.

▸ Software platforms for performance reviews and feedback, HR, hiring, and performance management. These are part of the backbone of any remote organization. Therefore it's important to remove human error from the management of those key factors. Currently, we use Culture Amp to support these needs.

▸ Tools that allow companies to collect real-time, anonymous feedback from employees and proactively identify ways to improve. In this capacity, a tool we've used for years is TINY-pulse. Real-time and anonymous feedback is important for remote workplaces. When you aren't interacting with colleagues and direct reports in person every day, it can be easy to lose track of how people are feeling about the company throughout all levels of the organization. You don't want significant issues like widespread employee unhappiness or disengagement to sneak up on you. Programs that allow you to collect constant feedback from your whole team are vital for helping you address problems before they fester and become bigger.

TEAM COMMUNICATIONS

Slack, Zoom, Microsoft Teams, and Google Workspace are perhaps the most popular tools that companies with remote organization use to manage their internal and external communications; they can also help foster collaboration and information sharing.

There are even tech tools that help add a social element to your team communications. Donut (donut.com) is an example of a tool we found that automatically matches and connects employees for virtual, get-to-know-you coffee dates. This type of tool can be especially helpful for more introverted employees who want to get to know their colleagues on a one-to-one basis but who are more reticent about connecting in a larger group setting.

Business-oriented tools can also be used to promote social connection within your organization. For example, our most popular communications channel in Slack is called #whatmadeyourweek. This is exactly what it sounds like: employees post a picture or a story about something personal that made their week better. This Slack channel was the brainchild of one of our employees, and not surprisingly, it has the highest engagement of any channel in the company.

PROJECT MANAGEMENT TOOLS

To assist with team collaboration and workload management in a virtual setting, it can also be useful to have tools that allow employees to see what projects other members of their teams are working on, assign tasks to one another, and provide detailed instructions to one another in real time.

While you don't need to mandate these types of tools organization-wide, it's a good idea to make them available to teams that want to use them and to offer them proactively as a potential solution. When teams can use these programs to manage project workflow rather than constantly emailing one another to assign tasks, clarify project instructions, and share feedback, it can help employees step away from email for extended stretches of the day without fear of missing important messages about their projects.

There are a wide range of options for this type of software, including Basecamp, Trello, and Asana. When entire teams or departments use one or more of these programs, it becomes easier to collaborate, communicate, and stay accountable to one another.

SECURITY TECHNOLOGY

In the event that an employee breaks your organization's trust, including exiting the company under acrimonious circumstances, you need to have safeguards in place to prevent them from causing any harm to the company on their way out the door.

Ensure that you have technology protections in place that prevent data theft, damage, or disruption. If your employees use their own laptop computers for work, an IT administrator should have access to every work machine to protect company intellectual property in case of emergency. You should also have the ability to remotely wipe someone's PC in case it is stolen or when they exit the organization to remove any company files and applications the employee may have downloaded.

Similarly, if you use a cloud-based file system, your IT team should monitor employee downloads to ensure they aren't, for example, conducting a mass download of company documents or data without a clear business reason. While you don't need to take note every time an employee downloads a file, many of the cloud-based file-sharing programs discussed earlier will flag suspicious activity that will prompt you to take a closer look.

Even the most trusting organizations need to accept the possibility of that trust being abused. These types of fail-safes allow you to give employees the benefit of the doubt without putting key organizational data, documents, or even functionality at risk.

I have pulled together a more detailed list of all these technology resources at **robertglazer.com/virtual**.

Technological Integration

This might seem like quite a bit of technology to manage, and for many organizations, it is. For others, though, it can actually help them reduce the amount of technological resources they have to employ.

Either way, it's important to consolidate these tools in a place where employees can easily access them and integrate them into their workflow. For this reason and to make adoption of the technology easier, it's sensible to specifically choose programs that integrate well into your preexisting infrastructure. The more user-friendly and convenient you make your tools, the more widely they'll be used.

As we discussed before, even people who enjoy working from home will inevitably miss social connection from time to time, and through technology, we can bring people together and help them share pieces of their personal lives with their colleagues to encourage connection and engagement outside work. You can also use these platforms to help with employee-led social events. During the pandemic, many organizations had employees volunteer to lead events and virtual social gatherings. At Acceleration Partners, several team members came together to host a show-and-tell event featuring employees' children and pets, group yoga classes, trivia quizzes, and more.

Managing and Leading

Jeffrey Katzenberg, former CEO of DreamWorks Animation, was known for running his hands on the hoods of his employees' cars when he arrived at work each morning to try to determine which employees had arrived only shortly before him.[3] Many leaders and managers put a similar emphasis on being the first to arrive at work and the last to leave. But as most company leaders can attest, face time is hardly a guarantee of performance.

I know this from experience. When I was in my twenties, I worked for a company that touted its flexible work environment and aimed to appeal specifically to parents of young children. However, the founder, who was not married and did not have kids, soon grew to resent the fact that he was the only person in the office early and at the end of the day and would occasionally make passive-aggressive comments about it.

Annoyed that the founder was focused on face time rather than job output, I tried an experiment where I came to the office before him every day for a week, then surfed the web or played computer games until my normal arrival time rather than actually working. I didn't produce better work, but I could tell he was much happier with me during that week and appreciated that I was there.

This experience taught me a crucial management lesson: having your employees spend more time at the office doesn't guarantee better results. In some cases, employees may even use face time with bosses as an illusion to give the impression that they are more productive than they really are.

In these cases, the incentive of "approval" is rewarding the wrong behavior. A better way to get the best from your employees is to create outcome-based incentives and goals that prioritize employee output rather than time spent in an office or on a task.

Leaders and managers who suddenly found themselves leading a virtual team during the COVID-19 pandemic quickly learned what experienced remote employees already knew: managing employees in a virtual workplace is an entirely different task but one that may ultimately encourage more leadership than management, to the benefit of everyone involved.

In a remote organization, managers can't walk through the office for face time with employees or see when the office fills up or empties at the beginning and end of each day. Team and organization leaders need to determine how to motivate people, track their progress, and hold them accountable at a higher level without constant oversight or micromanagement.

This is why we covered key cultural principles like goals and core values earlier in this part of the book. Once you've set up a clear goal-tracking system, it becomes much easier to hold employees accountable and evaluate a team's performance in real time. For leaders who are managing a newly remote team and wondering if their employees are still productive while working from home, this is a crucial measuring stick. When the company's goals and the employee goals that support them are laid out clearly and specifically, managers trust that employees know exactly what they are expected to accomplish and can hold them to that standard without micromanaging.

With this in mind, there's less of a need to worry about what an employee is doing on any given day or even how many hours they're working in a given week. If they consistently achieve their goals, those outcomes are what matter most; the inputs are less important. A big part of success as a manager of a remote team is managing people based on outcomes and knowing what day-to-day supervision is better off avoided.

Organizations that manage people by emphasizing the need for face time, long hours, or exhaustive effort do this because either they haven't set expectations properly or they are unable to hold the teams accountable. Clear, consistent, measurable goals and accountability solve both problems.

A challenge that some face when transitioning to a remote environment is managing projects without the benefit of frequent in-person collaboration. Managers who are used to stepping in frequently to assist their employees with their projects or to inviting a team member to their office for an impromptu brainstorm might struggle when separated from their direct reports. However, leaders can use remote work as an opportunity to improve their delegation skills and communication, which are crucial in any environment. Leaders can improve overall productivity and morale by giving team members the clear expectations and coaching they need to complete a project at the outset without lingering supervision. This is something that new managers typically struggle with early on; working remotely gives them more incentive to build this muscle.

Delegation in a remote environment has positive short- and long-term effects. When managers trust employees to accomplish tasks without constantly looking over their shoulders, those employees learn to find solutions themselves and grow more confidently and quickly in their roles.

Managers shouldn't be suffocating their teams or solving all their problems for them in any work environment. Unfortunately, those bad habits are often quickly developed in an office environment where it's easy to ask a manager for help at the first sign of a challenge or for a manager to see their employee struggle and jump in to help.

Performance Management

Managers at in-person organizations have always taken the approach of delivering important feedback, whether positive or critical, in an in-person meeting. This is especially true for significant performance management practices such as quarterly reviews, annual evaluations, and difficult conversations, including terminations. The idea of conducting these types of conversations virtually was previously hard to imagine.

However, remote leaders and managers must grow comfortable with these conversations not being face-to-face. Unless you are in a unique situation where you frequently see your remote direct report in person, such as at the same coworking space, these types of discussions are often too time sensitive and important to wait until the next time you and the employee are in the same location. In case it isn't obvious, it is essential to have all performance reviews and sensitive conversations over video call rather than phone, email, or chat.

For instances where you have to let an employee go, it is possible to do so over a video call without seeming cold or callous. Use careful but clear language to clarify why you've made the decision, and be sensitive to the employee's reaction.

Counterintuitively, this method can actually be less awkward than letting someone go in person. If you lead a virtual team and abruptly ask an employee to meet you for an in-person meeting on short notice, they will likely be panicked and dreading the conversation. Plus, being let go with a virtual conversation can be better for the employee as well—they are already in their own home space to process the development in private rather than having to take a "walk of shame" through an office, coworking space, or coffee shop after they learn they are being dismissed.

On the flip side, it's also a good idea to deliver positive reinforcement and feedback with more frequency in a remote environment. Because your employees don't see you every day, they may not have a clear sense of whether you think they are excelling. Be sure to deliver positive feedback shortly after you notice your direct report has done something well rather than waiting until their next performance review.

Psychological Safety

It goes without saying that remote workplaces have far less face-to-face interaction than in-person workplaces. Because of this, it's essential for virtual team leaders to create an environment of trust and transparency. If you can't see what your employees are doing all day, you need them to give you a clear picture of what they're accomplishing, where they may be falling short, and how you can help them improve.

Because remote organizations have less supervision, I've found virtual teams excel most when employees are comfortable taking the initiative and proactively finding solutions to problems they encounter. If employees email their managers for help or permission for every single task they do, it slows the team down and stunts employees' professional growth.

Leaders in remote work need to create an environment where employees are trusted to work with minimal oversight and feel comfortable communicating problems to managers who are literally out of sight without fear of judgment or punishment. This requires creating an environment of psychological safety, where employees are not afraid of making mistakes or bringing problems to their leaders.[4]

An effective way to create psychological safety is through your core values. Part of the reason we have **Own It** as a core value is because we want employees to be unafraid to tackle tasks and problems head-on and not worry about doing something wrong. We're well aware of the fact that this will occasionally lead to mistakes, and we make it clear to employees that mistakes are acceptable as long as they acknowledge them, learn from them, and do not frequently repeat the same misstep.

Remember how Garry Ridge and WD-40 referred to mistakes as "learning moments"? He's just one of many leaders realizing that an organization can excel when employees feel they have the latitude to make mistakes and learn from them. Ray Dalio, founder of the hedge fund Bridgewater Associates and one of the world's most celebrated leaders, takes this one step further with the concept of an "issue log" at his company. To this day, Bridgewater's employees are required to use this tool to log their mistakes for the entire company to examine so everyone can learn from the error and improve in the future.[5] Creating this tool clarifies for employees that Bridgewater is an environment where mistakes can be made in pursuit of proactive performance. In fact, while making a mistake at Bridgewater is not a fireable offense, failing to report one is.

We have a version of this as well. In certain situations where there is a meaningful mistake or poor outcome, employees are asked to fill out a debrief sharing what happened, what has been done to address the problem, and what can be learned from the error. We've even made a template for this type of report to make it feel as easy and as normal as possible for employees.

When remote employees trust that they can make mistakes in the course of their work without fear of excessive punishment, they will feel more comfortable working without the supervision of an office. As a leader or manager, it's your responsibility to help your employees understand that they can make mistakes, speak honestly about problems as they arise, and be part of the solution to those issues.

Keeping Track of Your Team

How do you keep track of everyone? This is a frequently asked question based on another misperception of remote work. The implication is that remote companies don't know what employees are doing or where they are at any given time. Skeptics expect keeping in touch with employees in a remote environment is like a game of hide-and-seek.

While we give employees the flexibility to set a schedule that works for them, that doesn't mean team members can just disappear for hours without notice. If an employee is running a quick errand or hitting the gym, we don't need to know. But if a team member needs several hours for a doctor's appointment, is taking the afternoon off, or will otherwise be unavailable for a long period of time, they're expected to communicate that clearly with their manager. It may even be helpful for team members to share their calendars with one another so everyone can easily determine when their coworkers are available and when they're not.

This speaks to accountability—during working hours, employees are expected to be available unless they've arranged otherwise with their team and manager. The expectations are similar to what would be expected in an office environment.

The same concepts apply to our vacation policy. We offer unlimited vacation time, but that doesn't mean employees can drop everything and take a month off whenever they want. An employee's vacation time must be preapproved by their manager and is limited in duration—unless there is an exception made—and we coordinate vacation time to ensure that, for example, an entire account team doesn't take the same week off. While we want team members to recharge and take time off, it's crucial for employees to be accountable to clients and one another.

No Spying

Having previously listed the technology resources we use to help make the work environment more productive, it's important to highlight one tool we don't use: spy technology to monitor our employees' activities on a day-to-day basis. While I realize there are some industries where this is necessary or required for compliance (e.g., financial services), we trust our employees until they give us a reason not to.

That said, we do have important protections in place should that trust ever be violated, including the ability to monitor any file downloads and to remotely wipe a PC.

Unfortunately, the marketplace has become crowded with new and creative ways for managers to spy on employees. The BBC found in late 2020 that companies manufacturing this type of spying software saw massive upticks in demand during the pandemic, including software that counted keystrokes, took random screenshots of employees' desktops, and tracked their mouse usage.[6] As a result, it's very likely to soon become a contentious aspect of employment and privacy law.

However, there's little evidence that employees are more likely to slack off when working from home. A study from Cardiff University and the University of Southampton, for example, found that employees who worked at home full-time got more done per paid hour than they did in an office.[7] Spy technology also creates a counterproductive cat-and-mouse game where employees attempt to outsmart the spy technology. Employees who know their managers are tracking their computer activity can purchase a mouse mover that automatically moves their mouse, giving the impression that an employee is working when they aren't. This is a zero-sum game, as it creates an additional burden for managers and an environment that lacks trust.

I was recently interviewed by two journalists from major publications who were working on stories about this category of technology. Specifically, they were investigating the huge uptick in software designed to spy and monitor employees during their day-to-day work, down to the keystroke level.

Both journalists shared that representatives from the companies who made this software insisted that it was a positive for organizations, that employees welcomed their activity being monitored, and that teams were more productive as a result of the increased scrutiny and accountability. When I asked one of the journalists what the definition of productivity they provided was and if it had anything to do with tangible business outcomes, he chuckled.

What these executives were essentially asserting was that their software was good at keeping people attached to their computers. I would be curious to see which specific productivity metrics have increased; I'm willing to bet that statistics like hours spent working or keystrokes have increased. While these statistics suggest employees are spending more time working, these input numbers don't prove that employees are actually getting their most important work done, and they do not take into account the real cultural implications. For example, if you were being surveilled in this way, why would you take the time to follow up with a call to a prospect for a multimillion-dollar deal when you can just move your mouse around every few minutes to please your boss?

Personally, I find it difficult to believe employees actually like being spied on by their company. It's more likely that employees are unwilling to voice their dissatisfaction with the practice out of a concern that they will appear to have something to hide. No employee likes to discover their organization doesn't trust them to get their work done. Spy technology may harm your company's morale and cause employees to seek out an organization that doesn't monitor them. I am curious to see how these companies' employee turnover numbers look once the pandemic passes and workers feel more willing to look for better professional options.

Being busy doesn't necessarily mean we are getting more done. In fact, I wouldn't be surprised if employees who are under surveillance spend time completing small tasks on their to-do lists rather than spending extended time on big projects that actually move the company forward.

There are better ways to hold your employees accountable for how they spend their time. This is where high-level culture elements such as goals and core values come back into play.

High-performing organizations are transparent about the values they want their employees to uphold, set clear goals and metrics that they expect employees to achieve, can easily measure whether employees are getting the outcomes that drive the business forward, and recognize that it's more effective to evaluate employee outputs, not how they spend their day.

As I asked when we discussed metrics in chapter 3, would you rather have a sales employee who works fourteen hours a day and never closes sales or a person who works two hours a day but gets millions of dollars in sales?

If you measure employees based on results, you don't need to worry about how they spend their time. That's not to say managers should never check their employees' work. Managers should regularly do audits to verify that what they are being told is in fact what is being done. For example, it's reasonable to suspect an employee is using their time inefficiently if they are constantly failing to get their work done and/or they constantly fall short of their goals. Those situations naturally prompt closer scrutiny.

Any remote organization needs managers to do basic quality-control checks to ensure employees are holding up their end of the bargain. Trusting someone and setting the expectation that their work and behavior will on occasion be verified are not mutually exclusive. This is why the world has auditors.

Aligned with this principal, a proverb we often tout within our organization is "Trust but verify."

If something seems amiss with an employee's performance, data is incorrect, customer problems keep popping up, or there are repeated mistakes, it's important to address this sooner rather than later.

When Trust Is Broken

As we've established, trust is even more crucial in a remote organization. Because one can't casually observe and check in on employees, it can be more difficult to identify when an employee isn't working in the best interest of the organization.

Leaders who are skeptical of remote work often fear that it will be more difficult to stop detrimental conduct before it metastasizes into a problem that can put client relationships, financials, or even the company at risk. While there's no evidence that remote employees are more likely to abuse organizational trust than their in-office counterparts, leaders in remote work can and should take steps to ensure breaches don't turn into major problems for the company.

Even companies that hire effectively and have a strong cultural foundation will have instances where employees abuse the organization's trust. This is not unique to remote work, but because that person is not working in your office, on your company network, it's important to have mechanisms in place that allow you to address these issues quickly and limit their occurrence in the future.

As noted in an earlier section, it's crucial for remote organizations to have a consistent feedback loop for all employees. If you follow the common standard of setting year-long metrics and holding annual performance reviews, it will be more difficult for you or your managers to identify potential employee problems early. In contrast, giving employees clear, relevant performance metrics that they are accountable for each quarter creates a more frequent feedback regimen and prevents abuses of trust persisting.

For example, consider a scenario where an employee decides, without discussing it first with their boss, that they're only going to work twenty hours per week, and their performance collapses as a result. It's far better for the manager to dig into this issue right away than wait for the next performance review cycle. They may even discover an extenuating circumstance, such as the employee needing to care for an ailing parent or child but being too afraid to ask for a temporary schedule change.

If this is discovered sooner rather than later, it's possible to both help the employee and repair the break in trust. However, if this went on for months, the trust violation would be very hard to overcome. A key part of handling trust breakage is building a feedback system that helps leaders and managers catch potential problems early, before they reach the point of no return.

This also supports the importance of aligning employee goals with departmental and organizational goals. In the unlikely event that an employee exaggerates their performance numbers or overlooks a key priority, it's easier to monitor performance and create strong accountability when their goals directly correspond to organizational metrics.

For example, let's say you're attempting to identify future managers and leaders in your organization, and you want your managers to spend time each quarter evaluating their employees and identifying which ones show leadership potential to build the company's leadership pipeline. If you simply tell managers to spend time doing this without assigning an objective metric, it's much more likely for managers to fail to make it a priority, causing the initiative to stall.

In contrast, if you set a concrete metric for each manager to refer two potential management-training candidates to HR each year, building toward a total company goal of one hundred, it's easy to identify which managers are contributing to accomplishing the company's objectives and which are falling short. This is especially true if the entire team reviews the metric each week and sets group accountability.

It's also much easier to audit someone's objective

performance when their metrics are tied to organizational outcomes rather than individual inputs, such as the number of sales calls made, number of outbound emails sent, or other employee inputs that are easier to exaggerate. Good metrics should act as a signal that tells you when a key outcome is potentially at risk and prompts a deeper investigation.

With the right outcome metrics, you should only need to take a deep dive into an employee's performance if something in their high-level metrics appears to be amiss.

We discussed in the technology section that it's vital to have technology tools to protect company data in the event that someone leaves the organization under strained circumstances or loses their device. It's important to reiterate that these types of safeguards should fall under your IT team's jurisdiction rather than being a responsibility for your managers. Your IT team can investigate anything that seems amiss with an employee's computer activity and flag those concerns to managers.

The final step to managing a breach of trust is taking steps to ensure these incidents are few and far between. This includes being clear with your team about when these issues occur and turning them into learning moments to help reinforce your culture. Begin these lessons by reminding employees what the company's expectations are, then digging into how the incident violated those expectations.

While we've been lucky that these incidents have been exceedingly rare in our company's history, they have happened nonetheless. In these cases, an employee has usually demonstrated very poor judgment, violated one or more of our values, or acted in a way that lacked integrity. When these circumstances necessitate an abrupt termination, false rumors and whispering can be harder to contain in a remote environment; many team members might not even initially realize the employee has left the organization, let alone understand why. Addressing these situations openly can help alleviate fear and simultaneously reinforce standards and values in a way that employees can understand and even get behind when they receive firsthand and not thirdhand information.

The last time we experienced one of these unfortunate situations, we addressed it directly in our next biweekly all-company call, explaining that an employee had very clearly violated our values and standards of integrity, resulting in their termination. Without sharing the details or the identity of the individual, we explained the nature of the incident and why it led to our decision. We did this not only to clarify for employees that trust and transparency are paramount to our culture—and that breaking that trust is a significant infraction—but also to establish how employees should respond in the future to a similar situation.

This is where a strong cultural foundation can help prevent

incidents of employee misconduct. In this specific instance, we wanted to make it very clear that the actions of this employee went directly against our values and that there were consequences, with the goal of avoiding a similar occurrence in the future.

If your organization encounters a case where trust is broken, it's best to turn those incidents into case studies and learning moments for the rest of the organization. This will demonstrate to your full team how much trust is valued at the company and how it can be preserved even after mistakes are made.

The fact is that many people don't commit breaches of trust at work from a place of maliciousness. We once had an exiting employee attempt to download a large number of company documents. When we reached out to the employee to tell them the mass download wasn't allowed under company policy, they revealed that they hadn't realized they were breaking the rules. While this may or may not have been true, the goal was to avoid these situations altogether, not to be put in a position where we had to question an employee's integrity or intent.

Similarly, on the next all-company call, we reminded all employees about our document retention policy that they had signed, explaining that downloading company documents on the way out the door was a direct violation of that policy and could create personal liability. We also shared that managers would remind exiting employees of the obligation and the IT team would be monitoring to enforce the policy and protect confidential data. Rather than attempting to catch employees in the act, we simply clarified the rule to avoid any uncertainty in the first place and discourage the potential behavior.

If you want employees to uphold organizational trust, it's important to clarify which rules are not to be broken and explain what is being monitored. Furthermore, by sharing trust breaches with your organization—without revealing confidential details about the employee or incident—you create an opportunity for your team to learn how to avoid these situations in the future.

The fact is that remote work isn't business as usual. It's an entirely different workplace model that will put your organizational trust and culture to the test. However, many organizations make this mistake when transitioning to remote work. They attempt to recreate their in-person processes and management practices in a virtual setting, whether that means using spy software to monitor employees' computers or conducting long update meetings where one leader speaks for an hour. In reality, building an excellent remote culture requires leaders to scrutinize which of their organizational practices don't fit in a remote workplace.

Vel Dhinagaravel and his team at Beroe didn't assume their in-person procedures would lead to success in a virtual setting. Instead, they questioned their current practices, considered what new ones they needed to adopt, and adapted to their new situation, using many of the strategies outlined in this chapter.

Through careful, intentional adjustments to strategy and tactics, almost any company can excel with remote work. What holds a company back may have more to do with the fact that their business operates in a way that is outdated and inflexible.

Remote work may seem like a challenge for many organizations, but it's actually a valuable opportunity for leaders to take an honest look at how they need to prepare their businesses for the future. Companies that are successful in the long term with remote work tend to be quick to adapt rather than inclined to cling to their existing processes and tactics.

6

Bringing People Together

There's a natural association between remote work and isolation. Many would assume that moving to a remote model would cause a breakdown in team connectivity and communication and cause employees to see themselves as less of a part of a team. This can be especially true in companies where only a small portion of employees work remotely—they may fear they are missing out on an enjoyable office environment.

This disconnection is not inevitable. Just ask Jason Lawrence. Lawrence is the founder and CEO of SalesFix, a Salesforce consulting partner with fifteen employees in Australia and the Philippines. Previously, Lawrence's team was effectively three cohorts, based in Brisbane, where Lawrence himself worked, Melbourne, and the Philippines. But when SalesFix closed their offices in March 2020, a funny thing happened, according to Lawrence.

"Our team are now on a level playing field. We have one team, not three," Lawrence said. By sending employees home from the office, SalesFix pushed them to work as a global unit rather than three disparate teams. Sharing and collaboration across the organization improved, and Lawrence's team even uses a video-sharing app called Remo that allows team members to see one another while working.

"My video is on almost permanently from 8:00 a.m. to 5:00 p.m., even when I'm away from my desk," Lawrence said. "The team can see when I'm there or not and can speak with me whenever I am as if I was in the office."

Even in a remote structure, Lawrence is still accessible to his employees. In fact, for employees who didn't work in Lawrence's office, he's perhaps even more accessible now. And to replace the in-office camaraderie, Lawrence and his team hold a ninety-minute video call each Friday where team members ask questions designed to get to know one another better.

Despite having his organization thrown into remote work under unusual circumstances, Lawrence thinks it's likely his team will continue to work from home permanently—they've already canceled their Melbourne lease. Counterintuitively, moving out of the office has brought SalesFix's global team closer together.

Connectivity and personal bonding should not be thrown out the window in remote organizations. Like all the strategies discussed in the previous chapter, keeping your virtual team connected just requires some additional thought and effort.

This includes making in-person connections. Though Acceleration Partners is a 100 percent remote workforce, we intentionally find ways to get together often, including client visits with teams and frequent conference and industry events in addition to biannual regional meetings and our annual all-company event.

In-person meetings and team building are crucial for remote teams. In fact, because employees so rarely are in the same place, it's important to make in-person meetings—for either small groups or the entire company—as impactful as possible.

Geographical Implications

Companies that experimented with remote work for the first time during the pandemic probably haven't experienced hiring outside their core market or office locations. The possibility for remote organizations to hire employees from around the world is compelling but also incredibly complex and filled with potential liabilities. Many companies that have started down this path may not realize the massive challenges and roadblocks they might come across. This is where innovation is needed, and the market is responding.

Nicole Sahin has built one of the world's largest organizations dedicated to helping companies hire and onboard worldwide. She is the founder and CEO of Globalization Partners, a global employer of record (EOR) that helps over one thousand companies in 180 countries hire globally. With over $750 million in 2021 revenue and several hundred internal employees worldwide, Globalization Partners is likely the largest EOR in the world.

An EOR is an organization that helps companies hire employees in countries where they haven't previously established an entity. They do this by establishing an entity themselves and handling the fulfillment of payroll, employee benefits, tax payments, and other logistics required for international expansion. In short, EORs such as Globalization Partners allow companies to hire employees in foreign countries without the time-consuming and often expensive work of incorporating their business in those locations and ensuring compliance with all local laws.

Businesses that look to expand throughout the United States, for example, face similar hiring challenges. Just as different countries have different laws and benefit requirements, different states have disparate laws and regulations as well. To handle hiring in multiple states, companies often turn to a professional employment organization (PEO), which fulfills similar responsibilities as an EOR but for interstate onboarding in the United States. In many cases, the PEO actually becomes the EOR and is able to offer small companies Fortune 500 benefits as a result of pooling together hundreds of thousands of employees.

These companies exist because of an important conundrum. Hiring in multiple states, countries, and regions represents an important growth opportunity for global companies, especially remote ones. At the same time, it can be a logistical nightmare to hire in a new state, country, or region for the first time.

A company that wants to hire a new employee in a new country without partnering with a company such as Globalization Partners might face significant start-up costs and months of work to prepare for having an entity in that country. They also have to arrange the appropriate payroll, insurance, and benefits plans for those new employees, in addition to tax and reporting obligations. In the best-case scenario, you have to invest significant time and effort in arranging all those aspects; in the worst-case scenario, you do all that work only to have the employee or market interest in that area not pan out. Then you have to pay to undo it all.

While remote organizations can hire anywhere, they need to have a more concerted strategy about where they want to hire and how they will navigate these challenges. Employers must be mindful of the potential problems that can arise when they hire internationally without careful preparation. Sahin has seen these horror stories firsthand and helped companies attempt to escape them after the fact.

Fast and Loose

Several years ago, Globalization Partners worked with a high-growth technology firm based in San Francisco. The company—which will remain nameless—was generating over $100 million in annual revenue and was gearing up for a big initial public offering (IPO).

As due diligence began in preparation for the IPO, the company soon realized it had a big problem: the firm had hired dozens of sales contractors around the world without establishing entities or the proper registrations in those countries. This created significant lapses in corporate compliance.

The salespeople had been paid as contractors, often through less traditional payroll methods such as PayPal, and as a result, neither those workers nor the company had paid the proper taxes in those various countries. On top of that, the company was violating many local labor laws through this full-time contractor arrangement.

As you can imagine, this created an enormous problem for a company that was on the doorstep of a huge public offering. But as if that weren't bad enough, the contractors became aware that their improper status threatened the IPO, giving them massive leverage. When the company attempted to negotiate with its contractors to make reparations and comply with all the required laws before launching the IPO, the contractors smartly used their bargaining power to make significant demands.

Imagine scaling a company to massive revenue and global reach only to have the future of the organization put at risk. This is the type of problem that can arise when companies hire internationally without taking care to navigate all the onerous, time-consuming legal work needed.

Eventually, the company and the employees settled their potential compliance issues before the IPO. As part of the settlement, the company had to provide major salary increases, tax-free stock options, and other benefit concessions. Globalization Partners helped manage this process and became the firm's EOR going forward, which facilitated a compliant win-win.

Fortunately, the story has a happy ending: the IPO eventually went through and was a big success. But the company invested over a year of time, money, and aggravation in the process, and they could have avoided that headache by using an EOR from the onset of their global expansion.

Saving Time and Money

In contrast, companies that choose to work with EORs from the beginning can not only avoid many of these issues but also accelerate their growth. A great example of this process at work comes from Magento, a top e-commerce platform that was spun off from eBay in 2015.

After the spinoff, Magento decided to aggressively pursue business opportunities in a range of global markets, intent on hiring talent in those countries as quickly as possible. However, Magento teamed up with Globalization Partners from the start to hire eighty-five employees in eighteen countries without having to establish local business entities.

Working with an EOR didn't just save Magento the legal nightmare that engulfed our friends from the previous example; it allowed them to onboard new employees faster, almost immediately after hiring them, allowing them to start serving clients and customers in those countries much sooner.

The ability to quickly onboard employees may not seem like a game changer, but it really can be depending on your business. Due to the rate of growth, Magento experienced a visible material financial gain from onboarding new employees even three days faster.

Later, when Magento entered acquisition negotiations, they sailed through due diligence without any legal hurdles related to their employment contracts, which had been set up properly at the outset. The acquisition went through quickly, and Adobe ending up buying Magento for $1.8 billion.

In business, taking the path of least resistance can turn into a huge problem in the long run. Rather than just hiring employees all over the world and leaving any problems caused through this to be dealt with later, it's important to be careful where and how you hire and to look to firms like EORs and PEOs or other specialists when you need expert help.

EORs and PEOs are on the rise globally, allowing companies to employ a small number of people in a new country at lower administrative cost. These companies are not cheap, often charging up to 20–30 percent of total compensation. However, they are an economically sensible option when you need to hire a small number of people in a new country quickly and easily without having to make the expensive and more permanent decision to formally set up an entity and assure compliance with a new set of labor laws. These companies also provide noticeable benefits to your employees. Both EORs and PEOs are able to pool employees from several different companies into one large group when acquiring benefits, allowing them to negotiate for better benefits plans for workers.

We have made extensive use of EORs as we have built our U.S. and global teams. You can see a list of examples at **robertglazer.com/virtual**.

The Hub Model

When we first decided to keep our organization 100 percent remote, even as we scaled up our business, we were open to hiring in any city, state, or country where the right talent existed. But we came to accept that this was too logistically difficult and an impediment to the world-class culture we hoped to build. It was hard to bring people together for our in-person staff retreat or for regular social interaction, both in terms of costs and travel logistics.

In our experience, we also realized hiring resources such as job boards revolved around local cities or markets. While it helps that many job-posting resources allow "remote" as a location filter, we aren't always necessarily targeting people who are specifically looking for remote work, and it's harder than you'd think to try to hire "anywhere."

We came to a solution called the hub model, modeled after the airline industry's common strategy, and I believe it's one of the secret weapons for bridging the gap between remote and office work and building a world-class remote culture.

To split the difference between a traditional in-person workplace and a scattered workforce, we decided to create a network of hubs, concentrations of more than ten employees in one location, and aimed to have 80 percent of our team in these hubs within a few years. While we don't have offices in these hub cities, we have collections of employees about an hour or so from a major airport to facilitate both travel and connection. We targeted hubs that had a strong supply of the talent we needed with a lower cost of living and where people were interested in a more flexible work lifestyle. This meant intentionally avoiding cities such as New York and San Francisco.

Sahin has taken a similar approach with her team at Globalization Partners, hiring large clusters of employees in hubs based in cities like Boston, Galway, Mexico City, Istanbul, and Indore. While Sahin's team worked from home during the pandemic, they'll continue hiring from hubs in the future.

Having employees concentrated in cities with other team members opens the door for coworking and employee-led social events. We don't force employees to socialize with other team members, but it's a benefit most of our people take advantage of and get value from doing. Most hubs host one or two events a quarter.

Having a hub model also enables remote organizations to conduct in-person interviews as a final step of the hiring process. We found that while video calls are great for the early interview rounds, an in-person interview is a great final check on social cues, personality fit, and temperament. It's often changed our perspective on a candidate significantly.

Twice a year, we schedule hub meetings where employees in

each hub congregate. We fly in members of our executive team, and everybody meets to have lunch or dinner, to socialize, and to discuss how we can improve the organization.

Because hubs are located near a major airport, our leadership team members can effectively sit down in person with the entire company in a series of meetings over a two- to three-week period. The proximity to an airport also makes it easy for people who don't live in one of our hubs to fly in to join one of these meetings. This system is a great way to help employees feel connected to one another, to build rapport with our leadership team, and to give real-time feedback about what we can do better.

The hub model is the perfect middle ground between in-office cultures and fully remote ones. It allows remote companies to build more social opportunities and connection into their team and helps leaders make key hiring decisions with more information at their disposal.

For that reason, Sahin and her team will continue to leverage the hub strategy, even as they transition more toward flexible remote work. Though the company isn't planning to give up their offices just yet, Sahin certainly intends to increase the organization's flexibility on virtual work. If anything, the hub strategy will make this transitioning even easier, allowing employees to work from home with more frequency while also gathering with nearby colleagues for in-person work at least part of the time.

Reinventing the Office

In-person connection and collaboration will always be part of work, even for remote companies. One trend we'll surely see as companies attempt to navigate a more virtual professional world is creative repurposing of office space. Some organizations will get rid of their permanent offices and instead use coworking spaces or short-term flex workspaces to host occasional in-person work. Others will maintain permanent office space but design it specifically for employees to use only for occasional coworking rather than daily work.

Perhaps unsurprisingly, one of the first major companies to announce an office reinvention is a pioneer of cloud-based file sharing: Dropbox. The tech company recently revealed that its nearly three thousand employees will continue working from home beyond the pandemic but will occasionally participate in collaboration or team building with colleagues in a communal office space. To optimize their existing space for this workplace model, the company will remove employees' individual desks and create what they'll call "Dropbox Studios."[1]

"In short, Dropbox is becoming a virtual first company," Melanie Collins, Dropbox's vice president of people, told CNN after the announcement. "It means that remote work is the primary experience for all of our employees globally. Because we know human connection is still critical in terms of building high-performing teams, we will invest in collaborative spaces designed for team-gathering and community-building, instead of a collection of desks you go to every day."

Collins clarified that unlike a hybrid workplace where employees do their typical professional tasks every day but simply alternate between working from home or working in an office space, Dropbox Studios will only be for necessary in-person activities like team building, strategic planning, leadership training, and other communal activities. While many aspects of office work can be replicated online, these types of activities will almost always be better in person.

This arrangement adds multiple benefits. Rather than having only some employees working remotely and experiencing fear of missing out on the in-office experience their colleagues enjoy, this will create a level playing field for all employees. Plus, Dropbox's new model gives employees more autonomy over where they live and work.

"Because of this model, with remote work being the primary experience, that actually gives folks more freedom in how they work in terms of scheduling but also where they work," Collins told CNN. "We will be encouraging relocation for folks with this new model. We want them to work where it makes sense for them."

Dropbox's case illustrates that remote work and in-person

connection are not mutually exclusive. Companies with one or multiple offices can shift to a remote model and reallocate some of their office costs into smaller, collaboration-focused spaces where employees can gather for crucial meetings, in-person training, and team building.

Earlier, we used the analogy of how moving from one home to another clarifies for you which personal objects and furniture you really value and which you are happy to do without. The same is true for office life. No matter how small or large your organization is, your employees really don't need to gather in one location every day just to sit on their individual computers, do their own work, and try not to distract one another too much. The truly beneficial aspects of an office can be magnified in a remote organization by making in-person time less infrequent but more intentionally planned out and impactful for everyone.

I imagine many companies will follow Dropbox's lead to give their teams the best of both worlds. Employees can spend the majority of their day avoiding commuting and working on their individual projects and tasks from the comfort of their homes while still occasionally getting a rewarding dose of in-person connection and collaboration. In this scenario, in-person brainstorming meetings or team building events will no longer feel like a disruption—they'll be an exciting opportunity to see colleagues in person and build relationships with colleagues they usually only see on video calls.

This is another instance where companies and employees pushed into remote work during the pandemic have a better future to look forward to if they choose to continue working virtually. For less money than they're paying for offices now, companies can rent and design spaces specifically for in-person bonding, collaboration, and learning. In other words, they can give employees some of the best benefits of working in an office without the downsides of daily commutes and office distractions.

Annual Summit

In addition to these smaller meetings, fully remote organizations should strongly consider an annual in-person meeting where employees can bond, participate in team-building experiences, and learn more about the vision and strategy of the organization and how they fit into them.

Most organizations—whether they are remote or in an office—hold some kind of team retreat. Ours is an in-person event called the AP Summit, where we bring all our global employees to one place for three days of training and team building. We invest a lot of the money we save by not having to pay for office space into making this event a transformative experience that bonds our team closer together and energizes them about our company future. Here is a sample agenda:

SUNDAY, NOVEMBER 3

All day—international and West Coast/Midwest arrivals as needed

MONDAY, NOVEMBER 4

10AM	Registration open
12–2PM	Lunch for arrivals
3–5PM	Orientation for new hires
5–6PM	Icebreaker/networking event
6:30–8PM	Dinner buffet
8–11PM	Evening social

TUESDAY, NOVEMBER 5

6–8:15AM	Breakfast buffet available
8:30–9:45AM	Opening session
9:45–10:15AM	Break
10:15AM–12PM	Keynote presentation
12–1PM	Lunch buffet
1–3PM	Team-building activity
3:30–5PM	Employee TED talks
5–7PM	Free time

| 7–8PM | Dinner buffet |
| 8–11PM | Evening social |

WEDNESDAY, NOVEMBER 6

6–8:15AM	Breakfast buffet available
8:30–9:45AM	Employee TED talks
9:45–10:15AM	Break
10:15AM–12PM	Leadership town hall
12–1PM	Lunch buffet
1–3PM	Team-building activity
3:30–5PM	Closing presentation
5–7PM	Free time
7–11PM	Dinner and awards ceremony

THURSDAY, NOVEMBER 7

All day—departures

This practice is common in remote organizations. The global web-design firm Automattic holds a seven-day Grand Meetup every year, congregating employees in locations all over the world. These types of annual retreats are partially dedicated to learning and training, but perhaps an even more important objective is fostering sharing and vulnerability among employees. For virtual organizations, this type of meeting is the only opportunity for employees to be with all their colleagues in a given year, so it's important to create an environment for instantaneous, deep connections and open sharing.

A great example of this came from our 2019 summit. We hired a world-renowned coach, Philip McKernan, to lead an event he created called "One Last Talk," an initiative he has run around the world. In this program, people come together and listen to speakers give the talk they would want to give if they were experiencing their final day on earth. Not surprisingly, this prompt compels speakers to share their deepest-held truths with the audience, even to those they do not know. We decided this would be an interesting concept for our summit. We acknowledged that there was some risk, but we thought it could bring an entirely new level of vulnerability to our team.

We asked for volunteer speakers, and I wondered initially if we would receive any. Surprisingly, we received eight brave submissions, twice what we could accommodate, and narrowed it down to four employees who trained with McKernan for months in preparation for the summit. These four employees stood up in front of the entire company and delivered strikingly personal and emotional speeches. Tellingly, these talks brought a lot of clarity to who the speakers were at their core and how they showed up for work each day. There were very few dry eyes in the room.

Perhaps most notably, I noticed these talks compelled our entire team to be more open over the remainder of the summit. The depth of sharing reached another level, both between people who had worked together for years and never had a real discussion and among employees who had just joined our team days earlier.

When you're working for a remote organization, these types of deep connections matter even more in building a great culture than small-talk watercooler chats do. I'm convinced events like this keep us closer as a team, even when we spend much of the year apart physically.

We also incorporate our guiding principles into the AP Summit, with a Core Value Awards ceremony that closes the final evening of the event. This is our only formal event of the year, where employees get dressed up and we give out awards to many of our top performers.

I explained in chapter 3 that our core values are crucial to how we operate and how we evaluate and reward our employees, and that's why we give out awards to employees who best exemplify each of our three core values. These are voted on by the entire company, and the previous year's winners present the awards. It's a really special experience for everyone.

Then, once we've recognized those core value award winners, we finish with something called a dream granting program, which was inspired by books like Matthew Kelly's *The Dream Manager* and John Strelecky's *The Big Five for Life*. We regularly ask and listen to our employees about what is important to them and also collect formal submissions each year before the summit. We then choose a handful of employees whose dream/goal we want to grant or help them achieve and gift that to them, announcing the selections in front of the entire company as the closing event of the AP Summit.

We've been doing this for three years running, helping with a wide range of dreams and goals. We've given an employee flying lessons, helped someone become a guest lecturer at a local university, and given sessions with a personal trainer to set and reach fitness goals. Some of these goals/dreams are even more elaborate. We once hired a private investigator to help an employee track down their long-lost brother and sent an employee on a trip to Greece so her ninety-year-old grandmother could meet her granddaughter.

This part of the ceremony is an unforgettable experience for the recipients, but it also bonds the entire company closer together. I'm always heartened to see how excited our employees are to see their coworkers rewarded and recognized. It's my absolute favorite thing I do in my role.

Paying It Forward

I want to share a last story of something we've done to bring our team closer together. It's an example of what kinds of connections can be made in a remote environment.

The story started when I decided to build a productive morning routine into my daily schedule. I had heard the value of such a regimen from a variety of leadership training programs I'd taken part in and decided to set aside time each morning for quiet thinking, writing, and inspirational, positive reading. The only obstacle I encountered was many of the inspirational books and resources I could find didn't have the intended effect for me. They were a bit too "sunshine and rainbows" for my taste. Like many entrepreneurs, I responded to seeing something missing in the world by trying to create it myself.

I started writing a short, inspirational note each week and sharing it with my team. We were, of course, remote, and I wanted to create something that allowed me to challenge our team to improve and pursue their goals, as in-person mentorship was largely not feasible at our organization.

I sent the first of these notes in 2015 and called it Friday Inspiration. They were short and simple, either writing something inspirational myself or sharing a story I'd found that week that was especially impactful to me. I sent them for a few weeks, and though I didn't think anyone was reading them, I really enjoyed writing them. It was the perfect morning routine: I was doing my writing, I was doing my thinking, and I was sharing it with my team.

Then I started to hear from employees who looked forward to the note each week and were sharing it with friends and family. Not only that, but members of our team shared how they used the notes as motivation to improve their own lives, whether that meant running races, evaluating their long-term goals, or even just improving their performance at work.

These notes resonated especially with our team because they were tied to our values of building relationships, always trying to grow and take ownership of life and work. But they weren't specific to our business, so it occurred to me that the messages could have an impact beyond our company walls. I decided to open the message to the public.

I created a newsletter system, bought a WordPress template for $50, and decided to send the Friday emails to a broader audience while archiving the old ones online. It began to spread through word of mouth as people shared the emails with others in their networks. Because so many people forwarded the emails each week, I decided to change the name to Friday Forward (**www.fridayfwd.com**).

Five years later, over two hundred thousand people in over sixty countries read Friday Forward each week. It's changed our business and my life beyond anything I could have ever expected, and it actually led me to writing two books, *Elevate* and *Friday Forward*.

Writing these messages during the COVID-19 crisis, I noticed an increase in feedback emails from readers. People were stuck at home, and many of them felt isolated, fearful, or depressed. Though these Friday Forward messages are simple, they demonstrate the ability to connect deeply with people even in a virtual environment.

I highlight this because remote organizations still have an opportunity, even though employees are not physically together, to make a connection through writing or phone calls or video. Those connections still mean a lot, even if they aren't always made in person.

A remote workplace doesn't need to be any less connected or human than an in-person organization. By investing in in-person interactions when possible and fostering an environment of sharing, connectivity, and vulnerability, it's possible to build permanent connections between colleagues who work hundreds, if not thousands, of miles apart.

Conclusion
What Comes Next?

When taking stock of the strategies and tactics outlined in this book, a natural question arose: are there factors—such as global reach or staff size—that make a company too large to function with everyone working remotely?

To explore this question, I turned to Bas Burger. Burger is the CEO of BT Global, a subsidiary of the British Telecom Group that has around seventeen thousand employees in seventy-two countries. BT Global sells technology and networking solutions to multinationals around the world, serving customers with operations in over 180 countries.

BT Global allowed employees to work remotely before COVID-19 hit, but they strongly preferred that they lived near one of the company's offices or customer markets. Burger's global team placed a particular importance on face-to-face interaction, both for internal meetings and sessions with clients and prospects. Many employees traveled constantly to meet with clients or work through complex deals with colleagues.

"The tendency for us, as an organization, was to travel a lot," Burger said. "We valued being together for face-to-face meetings. We had various regular events. Our customers, frankly, wanted us to be nearby. That's why we physically had to be close to where our customers were."

When the pandemic hit, BT Global was in the unenviable position of suddenly moving a global team to seventeen thousand home offices with limited time to prepare. While the circumstances were less than ideal, Burger was a long-time believer in the efficacy of remote work and was ready to embrace and lead the adjustment.

"I was always very positive about remote work. We have many, many professionals in our organization who like to perform well—and don't slack off. They're ambitious; they want to do well," Burger said. "In that environment, remote working just gives them flexibility, and it gives them choice. And I was very much in favor of it."

Burger affirms one of the core facts of working virtually— organizations of any size can adapt to remote work, provided they have the correct support systems and cultural foundations in place.

BT Global's international footprint was a double-edged sword as the pandemic swept across the globe. The company's offices in East Asia were hit early by COVID-19, but that early preview of the impact of the virus allowed the global team to transition into remote work gradually. By the time the company needed to shut down its European and American offices, Burger's team had had some time to prepare for the business's rapidly approaching new normal.

In some respects, the size, global scale, and resources of the company were assets that allowed the organization to adapt to remote work faster than smaller, more nimble organizations. BT Global saw firsthand how the pandemic disrupted businesses in China, and they used that experience to prepare for the pandemic in other regions.

As a seller of digital communication tools, BT Global already had access to the technology needed for remote work. Its employees had laptops, and its customer support agents used cloud-based contact centers that could be operated from home. Once it became clear the team would be working from home indefinitely, the only infrastructure the company needed to provide was simple office equipment such as keyboards, monitors, and other accessories. As a leading provider of cyber security solutions, BT Global was also aware of the security implications of moving operations from the controlled environment of the office to the fragmented reality of remote working, opening up a whole new attack surface for hackers. After all, this is something they advise multinational companies on—to protect their assets, their information, and, of course, their people.

At a glance, it might seem that smaller companies would have an advantage when transitioning to remote work. It's much easier to set up employee home offices, troubleshoot employee challenges, and create virtual communications channels for seventeen people as opposed to seventeen thousand. But BT Global's case shows that larger organizations have their own strengths when shifting to the virtual workplace—they already have considerable budgets for real estate, staffing, technology infrastructure, and global communications. The money is there; they just have to allocate those robust resources in a remote direction.

And while by far the largest company profiled in this book, Burger reports that his team reaped many of the same unexpected benefits from working virtually. The biggest, most unexpected surprise was how remote work created "democracy" across a large hierarchical and geographical team. Before the pandemic, BT Global was effectively a hybrid organization; many employees worked in large offices, and a large minority worked from home or satellite offices. Taking the full team virtual created a universal shared experience that previously didn't exist.

"Everybody who wasn't often in an office or was mostly remote loved it," Burger said. "Everybody was on a screen. Nobody felt guilty to be sitting at home. And in that environment, everyone felt that everybody was more accessible than ever. Things got done a lot quicker. At one point, we even asked ourselves, 'How did we ever have time to travel to the office?'"

Global organizations have become more prevalent over the past several decades, enabled by the convenience of digital communication and the increased ease of global travel. But companies of all sizes—including our own—rarely stopped to consider the true cost of all that travel before the pandemic forced everyone to reexamine long-held assumptions.

Once travel was wiped off the board, Burger and his team saw some clear benefits. Employees were no longer spending precious workweek hours stuck in traffic, airports, or airplane cabins. As a result, they could reach out to one another directly for help, and new collaboration opportunities emerged when colleagues weren't traveling every other day. The organization previously considered travel and in-person collaboration to be essential, but removing those elements actually made the team more effective.

To be clear, this level of efficiency didn't come automatically. Burger and his team made an intentional effort to evaluate and adapt their operational playbook to fit their new, remote reality, and they did so by leaning in to many of the strategic processes and tactics outlined in previous chapters.

Early on, team members realized they needed to communicate with employees more proactively to see how they were faring with remote work. Without the benefit of in-person check-ins, they needed new ways to monitor whether employees were underutilized, overwhelmed, or dissatisfied.

The organization also had to consider how to manage employee performance with a completely virtual team. Pretty quickly, Burger and his team realized they had to put more emphasis on results rather than activity.

"We decided not to monitor our employees' activity more than we did before," Burger continued. "What we do today is better manage outcomes. We measure the outcomes people deliver and, on that basis, determine whether we are utilizing our people well or not."

As stated throughout the previous chapters, organizations of all sizes need to emphasize outcomes over employee time and effort inputs. This should be the standard for all organizations, regardless of whether they are remote or in-person. Employees are happier and more engaged when they know what's expected of them, and companies perform better when they're able to set clear standards to which they can hold people accountable.

It bears repeating: this is a better method regardless of

whether your team is in an office or working from home. Working in an office, in many cases, leads to overbearing micromanagement; employees often feel pressure to work a certain number of hours, stay late, or work weekends. This type of in-person oversight is not possible in our current remote environment, and many micromanaging leaders are struggling as a result. Managers who are more concerned with the actual results their teams produce have had an easier time adjusting.

One of the silver linings of the pandemic is that it has forced many companies to make measuring outcomes a priority, as Burger and his team have done. At BT Global, they trust that their employees aren't looking for ways to avoid work, even outside the supervision provided in an office environment.

Paradoxically, many remote employees might be more inclined to look for busywork to prove their commitment and productivity. For example, Burger and his team have seen employees who are so eager to take on more work that they occasionally veer into less useful activities. Organizational leaders need to redirect this energy in a more productive way; otherwise, people will overwork themselves on tasks that don't even create real value. Getting bogged down in busywork is a lose-lose for workers and companies.

The pressure to appear useful and productive can be significant for remote workers, especially during periods of economic uncertainty. Remote employees can make a habit of holding inessential meetings or sending unnecessary emails to colleagues to show their engagement. Organizational leaders need to recognize this tendency and guide employees away from this unproductive behavior. One way to address this is to help employees feel more connected to their virtual colleagues. Employees feel less isolated when they have a chance to connect with colleagues socially.

Burger and his team have increasingly encouraged teams to hold purely social video calls. These gatherings are designed for teams and employees to bond as they would in an office, through coffee breaks, after-work drinks, and other social meetups. Working remotely has also made it easier for Burger to connect personally with more members of his global team, jumping into these "watercooler meetings" around the world in five-minute blocks to be present with his employees.

Because BT Global has offices worldwide, some of its regions will inevitably become safe for office work before others. Then, Burger will be back to leading a hybrid workplace. Even so, it appears that the balance will have shifted, with far more employees working remotely until the pandemic subsides in regions such as Europe and the Americas. This arrangement will present its own set of challenges for the organization.

Burger and his organization are currently evaluating the

best way to expand their virtual work strategy going forward. He's confident remote work will only increase for BT Global now that leadership has seen how effective it can be. In fact, the company has already adjusted its real-estate strategy to reflect its plans for more remote work, decreasing its number of offices and exploring converting offices into mixed-use spaces with both communal work areas and private rooms for virtual meetings with colleagues.

Burger acknowledges that in-person offices will always be part of the business world. People are inherently social, and many people are better able to tap into their creativity when brainstorming with others face-to-face.

It's also essential to consider that different employees will want different things, especially along demographic lines. Specifically, Burger predicts that younger people will be more interested in working in an office, in part because they are less likely to live in homes spacious enough to make remote work comfortable. These same employees will also be more enthusiastic about frequent travel, as they are less likely to have partners or children at home.

To make life easier for employees who do work from home, Burger notes that organizations should give every employee the best possible resources for a home office environment. Superior routers for the internet with built-in capacity to switch to 4G internet access if the home broadband drops, smart security services, dual-screen monitors, ergonomic chairs, and other workplace essentials add comfort to the virtual work experience, boosting productivity. Burger even added that there's potential for businesses to calculate the amount of money they would use to rent office space, divide that by the number of employees on the team, then reallocate that money to enable each worker to have a top-tier remote workspace.

Whatever course BT Global chooses for the future, Burger is certain that the company won't return to the way things were before the pandemic. In particular, he and his team are excited by the hiring possibilities available to predominantly remote organizations to go after the best talent on a global basis.

BT Global presents a clear example of core best practices for virtual work on display in a massive organization. While the shift hasn't been painless, the organization has been able to maintain a high standard of client service, productivity, and engagement despite having to transition to a fully remote workplace on short notice.

Furthermore, the example of Burger and his team illustrates the possibilities for leaders of remote organizations to build more global connectivity throughout their companies and to level the playing field for everyone.

Many companies historically had a structure where the vast

majority of employees worked in an office and a small number of employees worked remotely. In these workplace models, remote employees often felt disconnected from their team, certain that they were missing out on experiences and aspects of the social fabric of the organization.

In fact, many people's negative experiences with remote work come from this type of approach, where only some employees work from home. It's easy for an "us versus them" dynamic to develop, where remote employees think of themselves as a separate organization rather than as part of the full team. In many cases, organizations fail to consider how to help that small number of remote employees feel engaged and connected—both with one another and with their in-person colleagues.

Meetings in hybrid organizations can be especially awkward. While some organizations have attempted to incorporate remote employees into their in-person meetings by setting up video cameras and microphones in their conference rooms, this can cause more problems than they solve.

Virtual employees joining these conference room meetings don't see their colleagues well; as Burger noted, employees in a large conference room look more like dots than actual people. Sometimes, conference room microphones fail to pick up every speaker at the boardroom table, and remote participants may feel uncomfortable speaking when they are among the few people not physically present. Burger said he has suggested that employees all join meetings via their individual computers, even if they are physically present in an office, to incorporate remote attendees more effectively.

However, when everyone in an organization is in the same style of workspace—either all in person or all remote—this problem vanishes. Even massive organizations, with thousands of employees around the world, see a more level playing field when everyone works from home. Leaders must be mindful of this when considering their company's future remote work strategy: creating an environment where only a few employees work from home typically exacerbates the feelings of disconnection that can come with virtual work.

Nonremote Industries

I previously noted that *most* organizations can adapt to remote work if they create the correct foundation and processes. However, there are some industries that will be less compatible with remote work simply because of their core business model, at least until there is a transformative breakthrough in remote communication and collaboration technology.

Highly tactile industries such as manufacturing, utilities, landscaping, construction, and food services will never be able to become fully remote businesses. While many employees who hold operations, sales, marketing, and executive leadership positions in these companies will be able to work from home, those who provide the core products and services in those industries will still need to work in person. These companies need to avoid a situation where some employees can work remotely and others cannot—this sends the wrong message and can create a fractured, us-versus-them dynamic in the workplace. If these organizations allow some employees to work remotely, they need to set requirements for virtual workers to spend a certain amount of time in the field to build greater team trust, connection, and communication.

Organizations in artistic or creative fields may also struggle with remote work. While it's not impossible to collaborate remotely as a creative team, workers in fields such as architecture, design, fashion, art, and music often prefer to collaborate in person.

Finally, companies that do an exceptional amount of cross-departmental work in teams face challenges in a virtual workplace. As an obvious example, teams that work in product development will usually have an easier time working in person so everyone can be in the same room with prototypes and make collaborative changes together.

Building collaborative processes, shared understanding,

and shared identity on a team takes more time and effort in a remote setting. If your organization shifts employees into new teams on a project-to-project basis, the challenge of constantly reestablishing cooperative practices may be more trouble than it's worth.

While many organizations can thrive working virtually, leaders must carefully consider whether going remote is the right fit for their workplace and its professional dynamics. Self-awareness is essential to leadership; for company leaders, that extends to understanding their businesses' needs and thinking carefully about whether remote work can productively fit those needs. Diving into remote work without this careful consideration can lead to lasting consequences, so think carefully before taking the plunge.

Fly Your Flag

We have established that organizational culture starts with leadership, and leaders are at their best when they are self-aware. As a leader, if you're clear about what matters most to you and can confidently share that with others, that's a great starting point to build a thriving workplace. Self-awareness can define organizations as well. A self-aware company is one that has a distinct point of view, that establishes its mission, vision, and values and shares them with employees, clients, partners, and prospective hires.

As discussed in earlier chapters, employee fit is vital to a healthy organization. This is why I love a principle I call "flying your flag." As an organization, you should announce to the world what you value and how you work. People who share the same values will be drawn to your environment and instinctively want to work with you, and people who don't appreciate those values or practices will know that you aren't the right employer or partner for them.

Acceleration Partners has been recognized multiple times as a best place to work by Glassdoor, and although we've received plenty of positive feedback, I find the drawbacks or challenges people share—even in positive reviews—to be revealing about who we are and what we value:

- ► "Working from home is amazing, but don't assume it's a cushy job."
- ► "It's an agency, so it's fast-paced, which might not be for some."
- ► "You really need to be self-motivated to work in a company that is 100 percent remote."
- ► "Fast-paced environment with a lot of work."

Most businesses can define themselves just as well by what

types of professional traits don't suit their team, so always make it clear to prospective employees what the environment is like at the company they would be joining. In a virtual world, this becomes especially important; since you can't give candidates a sense of your culture by walking them through a beautiful office with energetic employees, you need to showcase your organization's core principles—including what you value and what you don't tolerate.

The Future of Remote Work

Imagine working in an office beautiful enough to serve as the set of a prestigious television show. For a full year, that's exactly what CEO Erik Huberman and his team at Hawke Media did.

The Los Angeles–based marketing agency was founded in 2014 and quickly built a team of more than 160 employees, developing a reputation for accessible, top-tier marketing offerings. To create a workplace that fit the company's quality of service, Hawke Media spent more than $1 million and two years finding and customizing an office space. Completed in March 2019, the office was stocked with state-of-the-art furniture from trendy office furnisher Vari, a conference stage for all-company meetings, private call booths, and sleek conference rooms.

"It was the perfect setup for how our business operated,"

Huberman said. "The whole thing just showed a lot of gravitas, and there was a lot of symbolism for what Hawke Media had become."

At the time, nearly all the company's employees worked in the luxurious office, and Huberman considered the space to be a key distinguishing feature of the company. The office was so cutting edge that HBO even reached out about filming the final season of *Silicon Valley* there.

Then, exactly a year after Hawke Media moved in, COVID-19 hit. The company sent all their employees home in March 2020 as the outbreak spread rapidly in California. Before the pandemic, Huberman didn't believe remote work was right for the company; he thought in-office camaraderie and collaboration were irreplaceable. But his employees adapted quickly, and the business continued to grow during an historic recession. More importantly, when Huberman surveyed his team to ask if people wanted to return to the office when the pandemic passed, more than 80 percent of employees didn't want to—*in any capacity.*

Huberman and his leadership team listened, and Hawke Media decided to give up their world-class office and commit to working remotely beyond the pandemic. While some leaders may have been tempted to push their teams to return to the beautiful workspace they'd invested so much time, energy, and money in creating, Huberman realized the importance of not letting the past cloud the future. Despite the considerable investment, he has no regrets.

"That office was exactly what we needed a year ago. And then the world changed," Huberman said. "You just have to accept that it's a sunk cost and get over it."

Organizations around the world are confronting the same questions Huberman and his team did: What does the future of remote work look like? Now that we've experienced a global experiment in remote work, what will the new normal be?

The answer is that flexibility will continue to be an essential draw for remote employees, especially for as long as COVID-19 continues to pose a public safety risk and a fear of cities and crowded spaces lingers. We have to remember that some employees who are at higher risk for the virus may not be able to return to an office for the immediate future, even after other employees have decided it's worth it.

Of course, some employees are counting the days until they can return to the office. However, others in the same organizations have likely learned that they prefer remote work, perhaps enough that if the option is no longer possible at their current company, they would prefer to find a job in a different organization. This may be particularly true of those who relocated from the city to the suburbs during the events of the past year, increasing their distance from the office.

As leaders or leadership teams, you will therefore have to decide what type of organization you want to build, considering both the needs of your specific business and your employees. Maybe you'll find remote work doesn't suit your company and you're willing to risk the drawbacks of competing with organizations that offer more flexibility. Maybe you've decided the infrastructure costs and rigidity of an office aren't necessary for your team to excel, and your entire team will remain virtual going forward.

It seems likely that hybrid organizations will also become increasingly common, enabling employees to work remotely as frequently as they want while still reserving a smaller office space for in-person meetings, collaboration, and socializing. This structure would capitalize on the hoteling trend that's affected office space over the past decade, made popular by office-sharing companies such as WeWork. Office spaces could be designed to accommodate flexible work schedules and meetings rather than assigned desks, as Dropbox is already pioneering. The overall footprint of these offices would be smaller, recognizing that not everyone would be in the office at the same time. A company of one hundred might design its office for fifty people, assuming a large group of employees will work from home on any given day.

Leaders who are exploring a hybrid workplace should realize that doing so requires just as much intentional thought and effort as creating a fully remote workplace. Hybrid work needs to be a strategy in itself, not the absence of one. Hybrid organizations must establish clear expectations and norms about when employees can work remotely and when they should be in the office. Leaders will need to plan in-person meetings and collaboration carefully rather than abruptly calling employees into the office without notice. Most crucially, they must ensure that employees who work from home more often than they are in the office are not passed over for opportunities and recognition.

An organization that previously worked in an office then became fully remote during the pandemic cannot just adopt the hybrid model as a compromise to make everyone happy. Company leaders must ensure that that approach is what's best for their stakeholders; it's important to create an environment that serves both the organization and its employees.

There is no right or wrong answer to what any given business should do next. But the strategy your organization chooses needs to appeal to your employees, make sense for your business and customers, and be sustainable in the long run from a cultural design and talent standpoint. Make your decision clear and unambiguous, recognizing that whatever path you choose will likely mean losing employees who either did not sign up for your new strategy or aren't excited about it. That's okay; you just need to prepare for change and clearly plant your flag rather than trying to appeal to everyone. Remember, the path that's least likely to lead to success for any company is the lack of a strategy or the absence of appropriate resources.

One thing that companies should be wary of is the sunk-cost fallacy of continuing on the same path simply because of the considerable resources already expended. A lot has changed with COVID-19; there have been fundamental shifts to entire industries and business models and a collective realization that some prior assumptions were incorrect. Just because you've invested a lot of time, resources, and energy in your office infra-structure doesn't mean in-person work is the best path for the future. Hawke Media's team certainly never imagined they would be happily walking away from their beautiful new office space, the centerpiece of their culture. Great leaders and organi-zations make tough decisions about what is best for the future of their business; they do not cling to what's worked in the past. It's important to make the decision for your organization or team with a forward-looking lens. Given all the changes we've seen and those still to come, ask yourself: what is the best course for your company in the next decade?

This is a rare opportunity in business; a massive number of businesses are facing the same fork in the road at the same time. Now more than ever before, there is reason to believe remote work can be a permanent fixture in your organization, with benefits from the standpoint of both people and other resources.

As we learned from the leaders and employees who shared their stories for this book, each group has a significant role in determining the future of work. It is clear that employees who want to work remotely will have more opportunities to do so in the future, and companies who assume they can use a fully in-office model indefinitely will likely face a dwindling supply of candidates for that type of work, depending on the industry. Many employees who have tried remote work for the first time never want to return to an office job.

Working from home allows employees to adjust the degree to which their work dictates other key aspects of their lives. Some remote employees have taken advantage of their newfound flexibility to travel for weeks at a time, working during the day and exploring new places during evenings and weekends. They've moved to different neighborhoods, cities, or even countries without worrying about commuting. The idea of living a life by design has historically been a dream for so many people, but working remotely makes that dream more attainable.

Even smaller-scale changes can be valuable—an extra hour of sleep, the opportunity to build a more intentional morning routine, the chance to turn a midday cafeteria break from work into an afternoon jog or yoga class. The trade-offs won't be worthwhile for every employee—some workers will always want the in-person connection of an office—but these benefits will appeal to more people long after the pandemic passes.

Leaders cannot be caught flat-footed as the world changes around them; supply and demand are very powerful forces. While offices in suburban or urban hubs were an accepted norm for decades, companies now need to consider how enticing remote work can be as an alternative for employees, especially as they age and gravitate farther from cities.

Throughout recent history, each generation has followed a common migration path from urban to suburban areas as they age, start families, and prioritize space and backyards over the bustle of city life. Even members of the millennial generation, who famously arrive late to milestones such as marriage and homeownership, are following this trend. According to the Brookings Institution, the millennial share of the suburban population is growing faster than their share of the urban one.[1]

This trend occurred even when remote work was possible but not at all common. Millions of workers made daily migrations from their homes in the suburbs to their offices in the cities, accepting the requisite commute as a sacrifice necessary to secure the space and comfort of suburban life without limiting their choice of employers. The expansion of remote work opportunities will provide lifestyle choices previously unavailable to many employees. Experienced employees in their thirties, forties, and fifties who want to move to the suburbs or already have can give up the commute, choosing remote work as a better fit for their lifestyle.

We should expect to see a strong push by developers and real estate agents to showcase urban and suburban homes with multiple office spaces, including soundproofing, natural light, and dropdown green screens, items that may become essentials for professional working couples shopping for real estate.

I believe we will also see a closing of the suburb-to-city bridge. People will still choose to live in cities, but that will be because that is where they want to spend the majority of their time living, socializing, and working. For those who want to trade city life for a suburban one, I suspect there will be less interest in making the long commute and more of a desire to work from where they live. This impacts a very large group of experienced professionals who companies count on to fill their management and executive roles. How will your organization adapt to attract and retain those people?

COVID-19 was an extreme anomaly, but leaders must prepare for the possibility that the massive increase in remote work was a glimpse into the future. They need to evaluate whether transitioning to partially or entirely remote teams will be necessary to compete for talent in the new world of work. Perhaps most importantly, they need to take stock of their cultural foundations, processes, tactics, and infrastructure so they can decide what they need to change to thrive in the virtual workplace.

While the speed of the remote work revolution is difficult to determine, we have every reason to believe that things are not going back to the predominantly in-person office of the past. Today is the perfect day to ask yourself: how do you and your organization want to fit in?

Embracing the Remote Work Revolution

You've probably noticed a considerable portion of this book was dedicated to best practices around cultural principles, procedures, and processes that all organizations need, remote or otherwise. The fact is that many of the core qualities needed to build a thriving virtual company are the same key attributes that all great organizations possess. Working remotely doesn't change these. Rather, it magnifies the strengths and weaknesses of the organization's foundational elements.

If you lead or work for an organization built on trust, respect, great leadership, clearly defined values, and world-class operational processes, all you may need to do to make the shift to remote work is invest in some of the emerging remote best practices and digital tools explored in this book. If your organization lacks clear core values, has micromanaging leadership, hires poorly, and operates in an environment of low trust and accountability, the transition to virtual work will be very difficult. For those companies and teams, no amount of productivity tips or remote work monitoring software can help you reach a point where employees are truly thriving remotely.

Times of adversity don't change our character. More often, they reveal the full picture of who we are and what we are capable of achieving. The same is true for organizations. You may suddenly realize your workplace has real structural issues that existed long before the pandemic, but these have become far more obvious now that everyone is working from home. For those organizations that want to remain relevant, that is where the real work begins.

We're at the edge of a new frontier for how we work. The organizations that lead the way and attract the best talent will be the ones that are willing to look honestly in the mirror and make the high-level changes needed to excel in an increasingly mobile and virtual world. The remote work revolution is now moving at an unprecedented rate, and even if that pace slows down after the pandemic subsides, I see little reason to believe we will reverse course.

In ten years' time, working in an office every day may feel as uncommon to us as flip phones do now. Our entire concept of where and how work is "normally" done may completely change. Throughout this book, we've used terms like *virtual work* and *remote work* interchangeably to describe working outside an office. It's possible our entire understanding of these terms will change in the future too, and we'll refer to everything we do in our jobs and careers by the same term: work.

Each of us has a role in building a workplace where everyone thrives. We might as well start now.

Notes

Introduction

1 Beth Braccio Hering, "Remote Work Statistics: Shifting Norms and Expectations," FlexJobs, February 13, 2020, https://www .flexjobs.com/blog/post/remote-work-statistics/.

2 Christopher Ingraham, "Nine Days on the Road: Average Commute Time Reached a New Record Last Year," *Washington Post*, October 7, 2019, https://www.washingtonpost.com /business/2019/10/07/nine-days-road-average-commute-time -reached-new-record-last-year/.

3 "Average Commute to Work Now Takes 59 Minutes: TUC Study," Sky News, November 15, 2019, https://news.sky.com /story/average-commute-to-work-now-takes-59-minutes-tuc -study-11861773.

4   "Indians Spend 7% of Their Day Getting to Their Office,"
    Economic Times, September 3, 2019, https://economictimes
    .indiatimes.com/jobs/indians-spend-7-of-their-day-getting-to
    -their-office/articleshow/70954228.cms.

5   Philip Landau, "Open-Plan Offices Can Be Bad for Your Health,"
    Guardian, September 29, 2014, https://www.theguardian
    .com/money/work-blog/2014/sep/29/open-plan-office-health
    -productivity.

6   Brian Heater, "Twitter Says Staff Can Continue Working
    from Home Permanently," TechCrunch, May 12, 2020, https:
    //techcrunch.com/2020/05/12/twitter-says-staff-can-continue
    -working-from-home-permanently/.

7   Chuck Collins, Dedrick Asante-Muhammed, Josh Hoxie, and
    Sabrina Terry, "Dreams Deferred: How Enriching the 1% Widens
    the Racial Wealth Divide," Institute for Policy Studies, 2019,
    https://inequality.org/wp-content/uploads/2019/01/IPS
    _RWD-Report_FINAL-1.15.19.pdf.

8   Greg Iacurci, "The Gig Economy Has Ballooned by 6 Million
    People since 2010. Financial Worries May Follow," CNBC,
    February 4, 2020, https://www.cnbc.com/2020/02/04/gig
    -economy-grows-15percent-over-past-decade-adp-report.html.

Chapter 1: Remote Working: What's It All About?

1   Jared Spataro, "A Pulse on Employees' Wellbeing, Six Months

into the Pandemic," Microsoft, September 22, 2020, https: //www.microsoft.com/en-us/microsoft-365/blog/2020/09/22 /pulse-employees-wellbeing-six-months-pandemic/.

2   Don Reisinger and Brian Westover, "What Internet Speed Do I Need? Here's How Many Mbps Is Enough," *Tom's Guide*, accessed December 14, 2020, https://www.tomsguide.com/us/internet -speed-what-you-need,news-24289.html.

3   Marisa Iallonardo, "Blue Light Glasses Can Improve Sleep Quality but You May Not Always Get What You Pay For," Insider, May 24, 2020, https://www.insider.com/do-blue-light-glasses-work.

Chapter 2: Getting the Most out of Remote Work

1   Cal Newport, "Why Remote Work Is So Hard—and How It Can Be Fixed," *New Yorker*, May 26, 2020, https://www.newyorker .com/culture/annals-of-inquiry/can-remote-work-be-fixed.

2   Anne-Marie Chang, Daniel Aeschbach, Jeanne F. Duffy, and Charles A. Czeisler, "Evening Use of Light-Emitting eReaders Negatively Affects Sleep, Circadian Timing, and Next-Morning Alertness," *Proceedings of the National Academy of Sciences of the United States of America* 112, no. 4 (January 27, 2015): 1232–37, https://doi.org/10.1073/pnas.1418490112.

3   Daniel H. Pink, *Drive: The Surprising Truth about What Motivates Us* (New York: Riverhead, 2009).

4   Liz Fosslien and Mollie West Duffy, "How to Combat Zoom

Fatigue," *Harvard Business Review*, April 29, 2020, https://hbr
.org/2020/04/how-to-combat-zoom-fatigue.

5   Manyu Jiang, "The Reason Zoom Calls Drain Your Energy,"
BBC, April 22, 2020, https://www.bbc.com/worklife/article
/20200421-why-zoom-video-chats-are-so-exhausting.

6   Avery Hartmans, "Tech Companies Are Starting to Let Their
Employees Work from Anywhere—as Long as They Take a
Lower Salary," Business Insider, September 15, 2020, https:
//www.businessinsider.com/tech-companies-cutting-salaries
-outside-bay-area-twitter-facebook-vmware-2020-9#:~:text
=Software%20firm%20VMware%20will%20start,city%20like
%20Denver%2C%20Bloomberg%20reports.

Chapter 3: It Starts with Culture

1   "Welcome to the Learning Moment," Learning Moment,
accessed December 15, 2020, https://thelearningmoment.net
/welcome-to-learning-moment/.

2   Brian Scudamore, "This Visualization Technique Helped Me
Build a $100M Business," *Inc.*, October 21, 2015, https://www
.inc.com/empact/this-visualization-technique-helped-me-build
-a-100m-business.html.

3   Robert Glazer, "Acceleration Partners Vivid Vision." Acceleration
Partners, September 1, 2016, https://www.accelerationpartners
.com/acceleration-partners-vivid-vision/.

Chapter 5: Setting Your Team Up for Success

1   Kevin McSpadden, "You Now Have a Shorter Attention Span Than a Goldfish," *Time*, May 14, 2015, https://time.com/385 8309/attention-spans-goldfish/.

2   Spataro, "Pulse on Employees' Wellbeing."

3   Benjamin Wallace, "Is Anyone Watching Quibi?," Vulture, July 6, 2020, https://www.vulture.com/2020/07/is-anyone-watching -quibi.html.

4   Laura Delizonna, "High-Performing Teams Need Psychological Safety. Here's How to Create It," *Harvard Business Review*, August 24, 2017, https://hbr.org/2017/08/high-performing-teams-need -psychological-safety-heres-how-to-create-it.

5   Richard Feloni, "Ray Dalio Started Bridgewater in His Apartment and Built It into the World's Largest Hedge Fund. Here Are 5 Major Lessons He's Learned over the Past 44 Years," Business Insider, July 2, 2019, https://www.businessinsider.com/ray-dalio -shares-top-lessons-from-career-at-bridgewater-2019-7?r=US &IR=T.

6   Lora Jones, "'I Monitor My Staff with Software That Takes Screenshots,'" BBC, September 29, 2020, https://www.bbc.com /news/business-54289152.

7   "Homeworking in the UK: Before and During the 2020 Lockdown," Understanding Society: The UK Household Longitudinal Study, September 14, 2020, https://www.under

standingsociety.ac.uk/2020/09/14/homeworking-in-the-uk
-before-and-during-the-2020-lockdown.

Chapter 6: Bringing People Together

1   Kathryn Vasel, "Dropbox Is Making Its Workforce 'Virtual First.'
    Here's What That Means," CNN Business, October 13, 2020,
    https://www.cnn.com/2020/10/13/success/dropbox-virtual
    -first-future-of-work/index.html.

Conclusion: What Comes Next?

1   William H. Frey, "The Millennial Generation: A Demographic
    Bridge to America's Diverse Future," Metropolitan Policy Program,
    Brookings Institution, January 2018, https://www.brookings
    .edu/wp-content/uploads/2018/01/2018-jan_brookings-metro
    _millennials-a-demographic-bridge-to-americas-diverse-future
    .pdf.

Acknowledgments

To my incredible team at Acceleration Partners, including Matt Wool and Emily Tetto, who have helped shape our company and culture into what it is today.

To Mick Sloan for his research and tireless and thoughtful editing of my drafts of this book, which was pulled together in record time.

To Richard Pine, Alexis Hurley, and the entire Inkwell Management team for their ongoing support and partnership.

To my editor, Meg Gibbons, for her continued support for my writing and new ideas. Also to Dominique Raccah, Liz Kelsch, Morgan Vogt, Kavita Wright, Erin McClary, and the entire Sourcebooks team.

Last but never least, this book is dedicated to my wife,

Rachel, and to my three children, Chloe, Max, and Zach. It is because of their love and support and their willingness to put up with me that I am able to focus on my writing and attempt to make a bigger impact.

About the Authors

ROBERT GLAZER

 Robert Glazer is the founder and CEO of global partner marketing agency Acceleration Partners, one of the largest, longest-standing, and fully remote organizations in the world. A serial entrepreneur, Bob has a passion for helping individuals and organizations build their capacity to elevate.

Under his leadership, Acceleration Partners has received numerous industry and company culture awards, including Glassdoor's Employees' Choice Awards (two years in a row), *Ad Age*'s Best Place to Work, *Entrepreneur*'s Top Company Culture (two years in a row), Great Place to Work and *Fortune's* Best Small and Medium Workplaces (three years in a row), and *Boston Globe's* Top Workplaces (two years in a row). Bob was also named to Glassdoor's list of Top CEOs of Small and Medium Companies in the U.S. for two straight years, ranking as high as number two.

Each year, Bob's writing reaches over five million people around the globe who resonate with his topics, which range from performance marketing and entrepreneurship to company culture, capacity building, hiring, and leadership. Bob has been a columnist for *Forbes, Inc.,* Thrive Global, and *Entrepreneur* and has also had his articles published in *Harvard Business Review, Fast Company, Success Magazine,* and more. As a speaker, he is sought after by companies and organizations worldwide on subjects related to business growth, culture, building capacity, and performance. He is the host of the *Elevate Podcast,* where he chats with CEOs, authors, thinkers, and top performers about the keys to achieving at a high level.

Bob also shares his ideas and leadership insights via Friday Forward, a popular weekly inspirational newsletter that reaches over two hundred thousand individuals and business leaders across over sixty countries.

Bob is the *Wall Street Journal, USA Today,* and international bestselling author of four books: *Elevate, Friday Forward, How to Make Virtual Teams Work,* and *Performance Partnerships.*

Outside work, Bob can likely be found skiing, cycling, reading, traveling, spending quality time with his family, or overseeing some sort of home renovation project.

Learn more about Bob at **robertglazer.com**.

MICK SLOAN

 Mick Sloan is Manager of Leadership Development and Content at Acceleration Partners, and the co-author of *How to Thrive in the Virtual Workplace*. He lives in Arlington, Virginia, with his girlfriend, Meredith, and is an avid runner, reader, and podcast listener. Learn more about Mick at micksloan.com.

Resources

To learn more about the tools, concepts, and processes described in this book, I encourage you to explore my resources page, available at **robertglazer.com/virtual**.

I am always interested in new ideas, partnerships, and feedback and would love to hear from you. Feel free to drop a line at elevate@robertglazer.com. I work to read every email and respond to most.

My Books

If you enjoyed this book, I invite you to check out my *Wall Street Journal* and *USA Today* bestseller, *Elevate: Push Beyond Your Limits and Unlock Success in Yourself and Others*, and *Friday*

Forward: Inspiration and Motivation to End Your Week Stronger Than It Started. Learn more at:

- *Elevate*: robertglazer.com/elevate
- *Friday Forward*: fridayforwardbook.com
- *Performance Partnerships*: performance-partnerships.com

The *Elevate Podcast*

Hear in-depth conversations with the world's top CEOs, authors, thinkers, and performers, including many of the thought leaders mentioned in this book!

- **robertglazer.com/podcast**

More about Me

To learn more about me, my writing or speaking, and partnerships opportunities, please visit

- **robertglazer.com**

About my company:

- **accelerationpartners.com**

Please Leave a Review

If you got value out of *How to Thrive in the Virtual Workplace*, I'd love if you could leave a rating and review on your favorite bookseller website. This is the best way to help other people discover the book, so I would appreciate your review: **robertglazer.com/review/**.

Courses

To learn how to apply the lessons I write about to your life and career, check out my on-demand courses. Learn how to create your own written list of core values to apply to your career and business, and see lessons on how to apply some key insights from this book into your own remote work life. See all my courses at **robertglazer.com/courses/**.

Read more
by Robert Glazer!

available from
simple truths®
► Small books. BIG IMPACT.